JAMES CONNOLLY

MY SEARCH FOR THE MAN, THE MYTH AND HIS LEGACY

SEAN O'CALLAGHAN

CENTURY

1 3 5 7 9 10 8 6 4 2

Century
20 Vauxhall Bridge Road
London SW1V 2SA

Century is part of the Penguin Random House group of companies
whose addresses can be found at global.penguinrandomhouse.com.

The author and publishers would like to thank Getty Images for the use of images within the book.

The publishers have made every effort to trace copyright holders but if they have inadvertently
overlooked any, they will be pleased to make the necessary arrangements at the first opportunity.

First published in Great Britain by Century in 2015

www.randomhouse.co.uk

A CIP catalogue record for this book is available from the British Library.

ISBN 9781780894348 (Hardback)
ISBN 9781780894355 (Trade Paperback)
ISBN 9781784751807 (Paperback)

Typeset in 13/17 pt Ehrhardt MT
Jouve (UK), Milton Keynes
Printed and bound by Clays Ltd, St Ives plc

www.greenpenguin.co.uk

Penguin Random House is committed to a
sustainable future for our business, our readers
and our planet. This book is made from Forest
Stewardship Council® certified paper.

'In many ways he [Connolly] was the master intellect of them all among the master intellects of his people, (yet) his mind often produced results that were bewilderingly disproportionate to the intricate process by which they had been created.'

Darrell Figgis *Recollections of the Irish War*, 1927

Contents

ENDPAPERS

1. James Connolly

2. Michael Collins

3. Bernadette Devlin

4. Ian Paisley

5. Patrick Pearse

6. Bobby Sands

7. Gerry Adams

8. Eamon De Valera

9. Jim Larkin

10. Constance Markievicz

11. Sean Lemass

12. William T Cosgrave

FOREWORD
by Martyn Frampton

Over the last forty years, Sean O'Callaghan has moved from being a member of the IRA to become a fierce critic. He has experienced the allure of Irish Republicanism and been appalled by it. There are few who have studied it so closely, with an eye for fine-grain detail and an understanding of the passions it can generate. As a result, there are few better placed than Sean to reflect on the life and legacy of James Connolly.

This is an important book for a number of reasons. For one thing, it is part of a general willingness in today's Ireland to look anew at some of the most ingrained myths of the nation's history. The spirit of 'revisionism', which entered the academy several generations ago, now enjoys a popular constituency. As reflected by the debates around how to handle the 1916 Easter Rising commemorations, nothing is now considered 'off limits' to the sceptical, inquiring mind.

Beyond this, however, it is fascinating to have someone of Sean's background and experience reflect on the meaning of Connolly. When Sean joined the Provisional IRA in 1970, few could have predicted that the organisation's armed struggle would outlast the Soviet Union and the Cold War. Perhaps the core driver of Irish Republican militancy throughout that period was a particular reading of history. Ruairi OBradaigh, one of the founders of the Provisionals, liked to speak about '*údarás an staire*' (the mandate of history), which in his view made IRA violence legitimate.

What he meant by this was the powerful sense that moved within the IRA, that its members were the true heirs to an Irish Nationalist and Irish Republican tradition that dated back centuries. The 'Green Book' that the movement produced in the mid-1970s – an ideological primer for new recruits – spoke of '800 years of oppression' dating back to the Norman invasion of Ireland in 1169. Thereafter, a powerful narrative of historical injustice connected latter-day Republicans with countless generations of Irish men and women who were said to have asserted their right to nationhood by force of arms. The events of the 17th century loomed especially large. As Sean describes here, the plantation changed everything in Ireland for ever. It left a wellspring of division and grievance that would echo down through the centuries.

It was followed by new chapters in the Irish Nationalist

story: the rebellion of 1641 and the brutal reprisals of Cromwell; the rise of Jacobitism and the events of the Boyne; and, of course, the 1798 Rising of the United Irishmen. Thereafter, a line of succession could be constructed, taking in Robert Emmet, Young Ireland and the Fenians. Finally, it arrived at Easter 1916 and the Proclamation of the Republic. The makers of that Rising self-consciously positioned themselves within history, casting backwards but also looking forwards. Connolly's comrade Patrick Pearse, who did so much to shape the spirit of 1916, spoke of his desire to 'lay down a book of law for Irish Nationalists'. In his inimitable, poetic and quasi-mystical style, Pearse offered 'the four gospels of the new testament of Irish nationality' as a canon for future generations. He envisaged an 'apostolic succession' passing down the flame of Irish Nationalism 'from the nation's fathers', until Irish independence was achieved.

This was the project with which James Connolly associated himself when he led his Irish Citizen Army to the GPO building on Easter Monday 1916. One of Sean's goals in this book is to explain how it was that Connolly arrived at this point. Often, there has been a tendency to see Connolly's presence among the leaders of the Rising as a quixotic, enigmatic move. Many have been baffled by the decision of Ireland's foremost Marxist to hitch his star to a wagon painted in the spiritual and poetical colours of Patrick Pearse. Was this a move born of frustration? A mad, reckless gamble out of keeping with everything Connolly had come to represent?

Sean offers a resounding 'no' to such questions. Rather than seeing Connolly's involvement in 1916 as an aberration, he sees it as the natural fulfilment of his career to that point. In his view, Connolly was a committed and fierce revolutionary for whom 'normal life' mattered little. At the personal level, that life had been defined mostly by failure. Connolly struggled to hold down any job and his passion for his cause exacted a heavy toll on his long-suffering wife and children. Yet he was, in Sean's view, a 'born activist' who dedicated everything to the revolution that he hoped to see in Ireland. From an early stage, Connolly was prepared to accept that this revolution might require violent methods and, certainly, he came to believe that the path to socialist salvation would be paved with blood.

Inspired by the works of Eric Hoffer, Sean presents here the story of Connolly the 'true believer', for whom 1916 brought the martyrdom he craved. During the Rising he mixed a curious naivete (believing that a capitalist army like that of the British would never shell private property in central Dublin), with a clear conviction that death awaited (he expected they would be 'slaughtered'). What mattered most was the fact that the manner of his death elevated Connolly into the pantheon of Irish Nationalist heroes. Above all else, he and his comrades became Irishmen suffering at the hands of wicked England. Self-consciously they offered their lives to set ablaze what Sean calls the 'emotional ethnic nerve endings'.

The remembrance of the Rising has been put to different uses. It was quickly adopted by the state and men like Pearse and Connolly were revered as the founding fathers of the newly independent Ireland that emerged after 1921. With the passing of the years it became ever easier for the Establishment to lay claim to the memory of the Rising. In 1966, for example, at the fiftieth anniversary of that seminal event, the symbolic geography of central Dublin was reconfigured with the renaming of Connolly and Pearse railway stations (formerly Amiens Street and Westland Row stations respectively). As Sean recounts here, that same year saw RTE, the national broadcaster, produce a deeply influential docu-drama series, which celebrated the rebellion under the revealing title *Insurrection.*

At the same time, the state struggled to control the meaning of 1916. Ever since the Rising, the memory of what occurred has been used to justify the actions of anti-state physical-force Nationalists. Within a few years an organisation had been brought into being, the Irish Republican Army, which was pledged to make 'real' the Republic that had been declared by Pearse and Connolly. Over the last ninety or so years the IRA has split and changed course; it has passed through a variety of incarnations. But always there has been a group, no matter how small, laying claim to the title and the right to engage in armed struggle for the sake of the Republic.

Moreover, the memory of Connolly in particular has long cut in different directions. He has truly been all things to all men. On the one hand, his involvement in 1916 ensured that he was recognised officially as a venerable part of the Nationalist pantheon upon which the state based its legitimacy.

At the same time, Connolly became an icon for those who wished to see change in the Ireland of the 1950s and 1960s. Under de Valera it became easy to caricature Ireland as clinging to the ideals of Pearse. Successive governments invested a fortune in trying to revive the Irish language and Gaelic culture. They governed an insular, socially conservative society in which the Catholic Church wielded great power.

Connolly by contrast spoke a different language. To many self-avowed radicals, he embodied a desire for change. His Marxism and internationalism, his commitment to women's rights, these all seemed modern and to point the way to the future. To many, this was Ireland's answer to Mao, Castro or Che Guevara. Sean recalls that reading Connolly set his 'brain on fire'.

He was not alone in being so moved. A new generation both north and south of the Irish border drew encouragement from the words of Connolly. From the students of People's Democracy to the Irish Taoiseach Sean Lemass, Connolly was a reference point for those seeking change. He has remained so ever since; indeed, he is the acceptable face of radicalism for (mostly bourgeois) revolutionary wannabes.

Equally, Connolly has continued to inspire the apostles of militant, armed Republicanism. When the 'Troubles' came to Northern Ireland in 1968–9, his name was never far from the lips of those committed to 'armed struggle' in the name of the Irish nation. After he had joined the Provisional IRA, Sean records his belief that he was fighting for Ireland and for socialism, just as his hero James Connolly had done. He was not alone. Hundreds, if not thousands, of others felt the same. Some joined the Provisionals, some joined the Official IRA; still others entered the Irish National Liberation Army, described here by Sean as 'pure Connollyism'.

All of them proclaimed their reverence for the spirit of 1916 and their devotion to the teachings and praxis of James Connolly. So it continues to be the case today. Though the conflict in Northern Ireland has mostly been brought to an end, armed groups remain at the margin, ready to challenge the status quo. And although small, today's dissidents – whether in the Real IRA, Continuity IRA or any other formation – continue to lay claim to the memory of Connolly. As the Irish state approaches the hundredth anniversary of the Rising, it faces the challenge of trying to honour that event without legitimating the narrative of those still committed to emulating its example.

More broadly, as Ireland struggles to come to terms with the demise of the Celtic Tiger and the economic hardships of the last decade, those who wish to see radical change are once more invoking the name of James Connolly. To many, as Sean observes, his words and writings have never seemed more relevant; in today's

Ireland, 'Connolly is alive with virility.' It is thus more important than ever that there is space to reflect on the kind of man he was and the meaning of his life. With this book Sean makes a critical contribution to a debate that Ireland needs to have about how best to understand and deal with the legacy of 1916.

As someone whose life was decisively shaped by a particular reading of who Connolly was and what he represented, Sean is uniquely placed to tackle his subject. As always, what he has to say makes for stimulating reading. What follows is a provocative and challenging journey through the life and legacy of James Connolly.

INTRODUCTION

O n the morning of 24 April, Easter Monday 1916, James Connolly, a 47-year-old Edinburgh-born Marxist and former British soldier, stood at the top of the stairs in Liberty Hall, the headquarters of the Irish Transport and General Workers Union, in Dublin.

Watching him was his friend, comrade and bene-factor Constance Markievicz, born Gore-Booth of a rich Anglo-Irish family. She later wrote: 'I had never seen him happier than on Easter Monday morning when he came downstairs with the other members of the Provisional Government of the Republic. We parted on the steps of Liberty Hall for the last time. He was absolutely radiant, like a man who had seen a vision. The comrade of Tone and Emmet, he stood on the heights with them, his spirit one with theirs. The rapture that comes only when the supreme sacrifice is made intentionally and willingly in a man's heart was his. His life of the flesh was over for him. The spirit life had begun.'[1]

At the bottom of the stairs Connolly stopped to speak with his trade union colleague William O'Brien.

'Bill, we are going out to be slaughtered,' said Connolly.

'Is there any chance?' asked O'Brien.

'None whatsoever,' and with that Connolly marched out to take his place at the head of the men and women who would shortly occupy the General Post Office and set in train the Easter Rising of 1916.

Alongside him going out to be slaughtered on that fine April morning was his fifteen-year-old son, Roddy. Markievicz and Roddy would survive the Rising, but Connolly, as he fully expected, would not. After the unconditional surrender of the Irish Volunteers he was tried in the hospital wing of Dublin Castle and executed in Kilmainham prison yard on 12 May 1916.

Unable to walk, having been badly injured during the fighting, he was carried on a stretcher to his place of execution, then put on a chair, his head tilting backwards, and shot dead by soldiers of the British Army, the army he had once served in. It is a scene that has haunted Nationalist Ireland and its hinterland ever since. 'The Ballad of James Connolly', which continues to be sung by Irish people across the world, recounts that 'James Connolly fell into a ready-made grave.' It is my belief that Connolly willingly dug that grave for himself.

At least 450 people were killed and 2,500 injured during the Rising, and nine reported as missing. One hundred and sixteen of the dead were soldiers, twenty-two of them Irish, plus sixteen armed and unarmed policemen, all Irish. Sixty-four Volunteers, out of a total of just over 1,500 who played some role in the Rising, were also killed. The results are clear: 205 combatants died, alongside 245 wholly innocent civilians. The dead were mostly Irish, mostly civilians, mostly Dublin's poor, killed for a cause they hardly understood or supported.

There is a simple reason why most of the dead and injured were innocent civilians. The leaders of the Irish Republican Brotherhood chose the battleground, then took over buildings that were mostly in the city centre, and invited attack. Dublin was a small city and some of its most densely populated slums were within a stone's throw of its centre. Did the leaders give any consideration to this? I cannot find one reference anywhere to suggest that they took it seriously.

Connolly appears to have believed that British capitalists would not bomb their own property, and this seems to have become a view common to the leaders. For instance, the sceptical Desmond FitzGerald was breezily assured by Thomas MacDonagh (one of the executed leaders) that 'the British would not shell the city, as by doing so they would be injuring their own supporters.'[2] Yet none of them could have been unaware of the geography of central Dublin. Connolly and the members of his Irish Citizen Army were intimately familiar with the area and must have known that it would be Dublin's poorest who would suffer disproportionately. Most of the civilians were killed by machine-gun fire, incendiary shells and artillery, so although it was the British forces that were directly responsible for most of the casualties, they did not choose the battleground.

It is just as well for us that two of Connolly's closest friends and comrades were there to testify first-hand to his words, actions and demeanour that morning. As I wrote those words it was difficult not to feel an emotional shiver of admiration, for it was those events that inspired my boyhood dreams. But those events also opened the door to the War of Independence between 1919 and 1921, the sectarian savagery in Northern Ireland during the same period, the Treaty with Britain that led to the Irish Free State and dominion status for twenty-six of Ireland's counties, the disgusting Civil War that followed, and the slaughter and moral degeneracy that was the so-called Long War in Northern Ireland.

So, for me, reflex sentimentality is quickly and coldly replaced by a hard affirmation that what I am about to write is necessary and urgent.

This is not a traditional biography. I am not by training or inclination a historian, academic or intellectual. This is about my relationship with the man and the myth that is James Connolly, it is about the politics of violent extremism and the blood-soaked legacy of what often passes for Irish Republicanism, and it is about the kind of individuals who are willing to sacrifice everything, including their lives, for a holy cause.

It is also inevitably about my own complicated relationship with Ireland, which is raw, visceral and gives no quarter, and is about as objective as it is possible not to be. I really am capable of hating the place as much as I love it. The fact that I can never live there again does not do much for my objectivity.

I was eleven in 1966 when we celebrated the fiftieth anniversary of the Rising, which was when I first became consciously aware of Connolly and developed some sense that he was different from the other Irish patriots we learned about. Prior to 1966, the revival of interest in Connolly himself and his Marxist writings owed much to the Connolly Association, formed in England in 1938, and to Desmond Greaves's biography of Connolly in particular. As early as the 1950s Greaves himself championed the establishment of a civil rights movement in Northern Ireland and, in the 1960s, he and former members of the Association played a significant role in promoting the socialist policies adopted by the leaders of the Republican Movement. There was also, it has to be said, a desperate desire by many disparate sections of Irish society to break free of the tyrannical legacy of 1916, the de Valera years and Irish Catholic Nationalism. In a slightly perverse way Connolly spoke to all of that.

Across the world today there is no shortage of what I have come to call true believers: young men and women who, like myself in the 1970s, are prepared to kill and be killed. Young men and women brought up in the heart of Western society who are prepared to fight and die for the most primitive kind of theocracy, who are searching for a cause that will fill the emptiness and the lack of self-worth.

This is the legacy of James Connolly, the son of Irish immigrants, who was brought up in an Edinburgh slum and found his holy cause in his peculiar blend of Marxism and Irish Nationalism – and died a martyr's death because of it.

Sean O'Callaghan
November 2015

Chapter 1

BLOOD AND EARTH:
The Plantation of Ulster and its Aftermath

Between Fair Head in Northern Ireland and the Mull of Kintyre in Scotland, Ireland and Great Britain are only eleven miles apart. Throughout its history Ireland has been both protected and dominated by its much bigger and closest neighbour. Ireland's desire for independence and Britain's desire for control is, I think, best seen in this simple context. I believe that this approach has much to recommend it, and for the purpose of this book it cuts to the chase.

Between 1579 and 1798 there were a number of foreign interventions in Ireland, ranging from Papal and Spanish alliances in the 16th century to interventions by revolutionary France in the 18th century. In the wake of the Reformation, the Protestant English were ever fearful that

7

their European enemies would launch attacks on their soft underbelly; a still largely hostile Catholic Ireland. Unsurprisingly in this light, the Irish were seen as a threat to be countered and pacified.

Displacing indigenous peoples with outsiders of a similar religious or cultural background to the conqueror had long been a well-used strategy. In his 1532 treatise *The Prince*, Machiavelli wrote about it at some length: 'One of the best, most effective expedients would be for the conqueror to go and live there in person... The other and better expedient is to establish settlements in one or two places; these will, as it were, fetter the state to you. Settlements do not cost much, and the prince can found them and maintain them at little or no expense.'[1] And the Elizabethan and Jacobean conquerors of Ireland knew their Machiavelli: Edmund Spenser, himself an English planter in Ireland and an advocate of such settlements, quotes Machiavelli in his own 1596 treatise, *A View of the Present State of Ireland*.

After the surrender of the Ulster Gaelic chieftains in 1603 and their brief attempt to live with the new dispensation, over ninety of them went into exile in 1607 and their lands were confiscated by the Crown. King James I of England began his organised colonisation of the Irish province of Ulster, intending it as a 'civilising enterprise' that would settle Protestants in a province that had hitherto been mainly Gaelic-speaking and of the Catholic faith.

The fact that at least half these settlers were Scots was

also significant. James I had been king of Scotland and he needed to reward his Scottish subjects with land in Ulster to assure them they were not being neglected now that he had moved his court down south to London. Settling a previously hostile land with subjects loyal to the Crown and to the prevailing religion must have seemed the ideal solution, particularly as the Scots had been migrating to Ulster for many centuries, and likewise the Irish to Scotland.

But the success of the plantations of the early 17th century was limited. Machiavelli might have approved the strategy of establishing settlements among the conquered, but he would have frowned at its implementation in Ireland. 'Men must be either pampered or crushed,' he wrote, 'because they can get revenge for small injuries but not for fatal ones.'[2]

Judged by this standard the conqueror was always going to have problems. The native Irish may have been defeated but they were not defeated fatally, and were capable of revenge; indeed, at times they appeared to think of little else. The conqueror, on the other hand, was ever watchful and fearful of the revenge of 'the black-browed tribes whose remnants linger still / with random beacons on insurgent hill'.[3]

However one looks at it, the consequences of the partition of Ulster were to echo down the centuries, leading inexorably to unrest, bitter hatred and a divided society segregated between native Roman Catholics and settler Protestants.

And trouble was not long coming. In 1641 the Ulster Catholics staged a rebellion, resulting in the deaths of more than 10,000 Protestant settlers. While the revolt was serious further south in Leinster, it was bloodiest in Ulster. According to A.T.Q. Stewart it was here that the Protestant siege mentality was born, 'as the warning bonfires blazed from hilltop to hilltop, and the beating drums summoned men to the defence of castles, and walled towns were crowded with refugees'.[4] For the next year or two the rebels enjoyed considerable success, and by February 1642 most of Ireland, with the exception of Protestant Ulster and a portion of Cork, was in rebel hands. The rebels were a coalition of the native Irish who wanted their lands back and the Old English who were loyal to Charles I. They set up a provisional government in Kilkenny and became known as the Confederate Catholics of Ireland.

Their unity and independence did not last long. In August 1649, determined to assert his authority and punish the rebels, Oliver Cromwell landed in Ireland. Cromwell was merciless in his pursuit of success, and for many in Ireland his name has become a byword for wanton cruelty. His methods mirrored military tactics common at the time, and by the summer of 1652 the whole country had submitted to his rule. Yet even then Ireland remained far from settled.

When William of Orange landed in England in 1688 to seize the throne, his father-in-law, James II, fled first to France and then to Ireland, where he prepared to launch a counter-attack to reclaim his crown. However, other than holding a parliament in Dublin and transferring land to the native Irish, James was largely inactive in Ireland – until William landed in Carrickfergus in 1690 and James decided to confront him at the River Boyne. The subsequent victory for William at the Battle of the Boyne is still celebrated annually by many thousands of Protestants, mainly in Northern Ireland and Scotland. In 1691 Irish resistance largely came to an end with the signing of the Treaty of Limerick.

In the years that followed there was little appetite for further revolt in Ireland and many Jacobites (supporters of James II and his heirs) left to join Continental armies, especially in France, where it has been estimated that at least half a million Irishmen joined the French Army between 1691 and 1791.

Ireland's peaceful 18th century was brought to an end by the wave of instability unleashed by the French Revolution. Events in Paris had a considerable impact on Irish public opinion and raised hopes of religious freedom and an extension of the franchise. Most significantly the Society of United Irishmen was formed in Belfast in 1791, mainly by Presbyterian and Anglican intellectuals such as Wolfe Tone. Inspired by the French example and preaching of Liberty, Equality and Fraternity, it hoped to unite Catholic, Protestant and Dissenters under the common name of Irishmen to break the connection with England, and in 1798 a new rebellion was launched.

Famously, they were defeated, and Wolfe Tone, the

Anglican leader of the United Irishmen, was captured on Lough Swilly awaiting a French expeditionary force. Regarded as the founder of Irish Republicanism, he committed suicide in his prison cell rather than face the ignominy of death by hanging.

More broadly, the rebellion of 1798 was a disaster for Ireland. The mainly Presbyterian (or Dissenter) leaders of the United Irishmen may have been true believers in their revolutionary ideals, but others within their movement were animated by rather less lofty sentiments. The primarily Catholic peasantry looked to Catholic France as the enemy of Protestant England. They also wanted to destroy their landlords, most of whom were Protestant. As Conor Cruise O'Brien wrote: 'These are conditions in which it is hard to tell class war from religious or tribal war, and hard even for those involved to be sure which it is that they are at.'[5]

The events of 1798 left the non-sectarian principles of the United Irishmen in tatters. In County Wexford, for example, the rebellion was little more than a nakedly sectarian confrontation. In one incident more than 100 Protestants were burned to death in a barn at Scullabogue; in another, on 20 June in Wexford town, seventy Protestants were executed on a bridge spanning the River Slaney.

The rebellion was eventually savagely suppressed; about 30,000 people died and atrocities were committed on both sides. The United Irishmen were destroyed and their lofty ideals discredited, the result of which was that the existing divisions of race and faith within Ireland were deepened.

In spite of this, a belief in the utility of violent insurrection did not die with the failures of 1798. In 1803 there was a tiny and hopelessly bungled rebellion led by Robert Emmet, a kind of postscript to the events of five years earlier, and Emmet himself was duly hanged.

By the time of the abortive rising of 1803 Ireland's constitutional position had been transformed in that, ironically, the actual result of the 1798 rebellion was almost the exact opposite of what it had intended. Rather than securing the separation of Ireland from England, the rebellion helped to pave the way for the Act of Union in January 1801. The Irish parliament, known as Grattan's Parliament, was abolished (in truth, it had held little real power), and Ireland was incorporated formally into the new state of the United Kingdom of Great Britain and Ireland. From now on Ireland would be represented at Westminster by 100 MPs and thirty-two peers.

Originally the Act of Union was to be accompanied by a bill of emancipation for Catholics. Long-established legal provisions that discriminated against them and made them second-class citizens were to be abolished. Unfortunately, however, this part of the Union project proved stillborn, and as time went by Catholics continued to face various disadvantages. In the early years of the 19th century, for example, Catholics could still not sit in

Parliament, even though Catholic votes now sent many representatives to Westminster; neither could they hold senior positions in the military, civil service or judiciary.

The arrival of the Irish lawyer Daniel O'Connell on the scene began the process that changed all that. Using a mix of non-violent protest and parliamentary pressure O'Connell succeeded in forcing the government to introduce the Roman Catholic Relief Act in 1829. In 1841 O'Connell, now an MP and totally opposed to bloodshed, decided to launch another campaign for the repeal of the Union between Ireland and England. This time he met with implacable government opposition. Rather than risk violence O'Connell backed down and thus lost face, particularly with the younger radical elements represented by the Young Ireland movement. The writings of a fringe member of this group, James Fintan Lalor, on the land question would greatly influence James Connolly.

Between 1845 and 1849 Ireland was devastated by the Great Famine in which a million people died and a million more emigrated, almost all of whom (the dead and the migrants) were Catholics. Depressed by the failure to break the Union and enraged by the Famine, the leaders of the Young Irelanders tried to stage a rebellion in 1848, but it was a hopeless disaster. The Famine also served to greatly increase hatred of British rule, both among those left in Ireland and those who made it to America, where, if anything, it strengthened in intensity as the folk stories handed down from generation to generation grew ever more lurid.

In my opinion, the road that was to lead to the 1916 Rising and beyond belonged as much to America as it did to Ireland. On St Patrick's Day 1858 the Irish Republican Brotherhood was formed in Dublin by James Stephens, a veteran of the Young Ireland movement. A secret-oath-bound revolutionary society, it is best known by the name it adopted in America: the Fenians. A rising was attempted in 1867, but the authorities moved early, arresting many of the leaders, and it turned out to be yet another damp squib. In military terms they were utterly unsuccessful, but some of their leaders were bright, imaginative and determined, among them John Devoy in America (the Irish-American lynchpin of the 1916 Rising) and Michael Davitt in Ireland, who along with Charles Stewart Parnell moved their focus on from direct action and helped create the New Departure, a socio-political movement of astonishing effectiveness. Launched in the late-1870s, the mass formation of this movement became the Irish National Land League, which was to be another major influence on James Connolly and his generation.

At the same time, the lure of political violence was never far away. Not everyone in the Fenian movement was ready to embrace purely peaceful means. The 1880s witnessed the first sustained campaign of terrorism waged against the British mainland by those who claimed to speak for Ireland. Public buildings, among them Scotland

Yard, and other utilities were targeted for dynamite attacks. From across the Atlantic these 'skirmishers' were encouraged and funded by the growing community of Irish-Americans and Irish exiles. The voice of Jeremiah O'Donovan Rossa was one of the loudest, demanding relentless attacks on the English enemy. In 1882 a shocking act of violence saw the slaughter, by knife, of Lord Frederick C. Cavendish, newly appointed chief secretary for Ireland, and Thomas Henry Burke, the permanent under-secretary, as they were walking through Phoenix Park in Dublin. The perpetrators were arrested and hanged. But the murders marked another grim milestone in the fight for Irish independence.

Looking back on this necessarily potted history several things stand out. One is the enduring appeal of violent methods to those Irishmen who wished to break the connection with England. Equally it is hard not to see that such endeavours only ended in failure and, indeed, tended to bring consequences almost diametrically opposed to the objectives of the rebels.

Why was this? From 1798 onwards no separatist movement or conspiracy in Ireland enjoyed anything like majority support for violent revolt against British rule. The Plantation of Ulster had also changed life in Ireland for ever, ending Catholic Gaelic hegemony in the north-east of the province where the dominant political, economic and numerical power was now held by people of a fundamentally different religion, fealty and culture.

Mainly Protestant and loyal to the Crown, they were to become ever more wary and fearful of revenge attacks from the dispossessed Catholics, who perhaps understandably resented them deeply.

'Since those distant days,' Cruise O'Brien writes, 'the outlines of the problem have shifted many times, but the 17th-century settlement was so massive and vital a fact that its original character continues to dominate every aspect of the life of the region affected, and to permeate the politics of the whole island.'[6]

An experience of my own illustrates this. In 1974 I was standing with an old farmer on a hillside in County Tyrone while he pointed out Protestant farms 'stolen from us by them black bastards'. Here, I understood, was the emotive power of blood and earth.[7]

Chapter 2

A DEFEATED PEOPLE

James Connolly was born in Edinburgh of Irish parents on 5 June 1868. John Connolly and Mary McGinn, were both Irish Catholics from County Monaghan in Ulster. Like many others they left Ireland in the years after the Famine to seek a new life elsewhere. Because of its proximity to Ulster, Scotland was almost certainly the easiest and cheapest place for them to go, and the records show that they were married by Father O'Donnell in Edinburgh on 20 October 1856.

By the time James Connolly was born the couple already had two boys, John and Thomas. We will hear more of John, the eldest, whose footsteps the younger James would often follow. Of Thomas there is very little recorded. Home was the Cowgate, known locally as 'Little Ireland', an Irish-Catholic ghetto in the Old Town, within walking distance of Edinburgh University. In 1868 it was a festering, disease-ridden slum of over 14,000 mostly Irish immigrant Catholics who were not entirely loved or wanted in the city of John Knox. In 1866 John Symington wrote: 'The atmosphere is fouly tainted, and rendered almost unendurable by its loathsomeness at those periods when offal and nuisance require to be deposited on the streets.'[1]

John Connolly was employed for much of his life in Edinburgh as a manure carter, which meant he collected human and household waste for the city corporation. An event in 1861 may have later been recounted to James by his father. That year the manure carters threatened strike action unless their conditions were improved. After a hastily convened meeting of the relevant council section it was agreed that their demands should be met. It appears that this successful action by unskilled Irish-Catholic workers became the stuff of near legend in Cowgate. It is not known whether John Connolly played a major role, but stories such as this would have inspired James and his elder brother John to take up rebellious causes themselves. Both would later become active in socialist politics in Scotland.

Their father's position was full time, but after an accident in his mid-fifties he was put in charge of a public toilet. Mary Connolly suffered very poor health for much of her adult life, and this may explain the long gaps between the births of the three brothers. According to C. Desmond Greaves in his biography of James Connolly, she fell ill with chronic bronchitis following the birth of her first child on 31 January 1862 which she suffered from until her death thirty years later. Suffering from chronic bronchitis in the appalling conditions of Cowgate in the mid nineteenth century, and for over thirty years, must have been a horrible way to live and die.

We have only what is, in my view, the unreliable testimony of James Connolly's daughter Nora as to his relationship with his father. Did he ever speak or write of his parents in any detail? It would appear not. Until Greaves was able to prove that Connolly was born in Edinburgh and served in the British Army, many accounts of his early life were a fiction, and included claims that he was born in County Monaghan and never enlisted in the army. Connolly added to the confusion by stating on a 1901 census form in Dublin that County Monaghan was his birthplace, and he never openly admitted to his service in the British Army, partly because he was a deserter but also because most of his service had been in Ireland.

What is certain is that all three Connolly brothers left not only Cowgate but Scotland itself as soon as they could. This might reflect unhappiness at home, or a need to improve their lives, a desire for adventure, or a combination of all these factors. None of this is known because Connolly never wrote about his early life.

Are these things important? To understand the motivations behind many of Connolly's subsequent decisions and actions, I would say yes. He demanded a lot from

others, not least his wife and family, and from those who
followed him, as well as those who didn't but died none
the less on the streets of Dublin in 1916. I believe it is
legitimate to ask hard questions of James Connolly.
Anyone who demands great sacrifice from others must
surely expect their record to be judged at some time in
the future.

There can be no doubt that growing up in Cowgate
branded both class consciousness and Irish Nationalism
into Connolly's soul. It was a time and place of terrible
degradation, poverty and daily humiliation. The one thing
that distinguishes Cowgate from run-of-the-mill poverty
in other working-class areas is that it was also an
Irish-Catholic slum with a collective sense of injustice
that was not solely class based. Sectarian attacks on the
inhabitants of 'Little Ireland' were not uncommon in the
earlier part of the 19th century, although they seem to
have run their course by the time the young James came
along.

These Catholic Irish were a defeated people who had
left their homes to seek a new life in the land of the
conqueror. The songs, the stories, the exaggerated or
invented tales of power and influence at home festered
and called for revenge against the oppressor. Their living
conditions were terrible, their lives were hard and, with
a chronically ill mother, the Connollys had it tougher
than most. But the father had employment and his sons
worked too. Before too long John and James enlisted in
the army, and Thomas emigrated, having acquired, it

would seem, the rudiments of a trade in the printing world. How bad was it growing up and living in Cowgate? Without written evidence we can only speculate, although he bore physical reminders from that period: a squint, acquired by his own account from reading by the light of burning embers; and bow legs, most likely caused by childhood rickets, and a stutter, which he all but conquered in adult life. These scars were an embodiment of the sense of powerlessness and resentment which were to drive Connolly for the rest of his life.

But life in Edinburgh was little different in material terms from the poverty of working-class Dublin, London or Manchester. I say this because we Irish have a tendency to regard ourselves as the 'most oppressed people ever', an acronym coined by Professor Liam Kennedy of Queen's University as the MOPE syndrome. That Connolly suffered uniquely as a child of Cowgate and that this inevitably set him on the road to rebellion and eventual execution may be a myth, but it has added potency to a story of ethnic resentment which has bedevilled Nationalist Ireland for generations.

In any case, Connolly came out of Cowgate raging against the world. He was a man of great intelligence and ability who never got over his sense of being owed. He was also a great hater who fought against everyone and everything. This argumentative nature would take him in and out of trade union's/socialist parties in Scotland, Ireland and America throughout his life.

He also possessed the ugly sentimentality of the true

absolutist, and only the selfless pursuit of his holy cause, the global Workers' Republic, that shining city on the hill, could satisfy the demon within. Ultimately it would kill him and, directly or indirectly, many others who had never heard of Karl Marx and had no wish to die for some utopian ideal. And it seemed to be a life mostly without joy. 'As long as I live I will have no rest,' he declared, 'only working, educating, organising and fighting to destroy the forces that produce poverty.'[2]

As a young man I admired this kind of commitment. Now I find it ugly, sad and empty of what it is to be truly human.

The three Connolly brothers all attended St Patrick's School in Cowgate, where they received no more than a rudimentary education, finishing at the age of ten or eleven. James's first job on leaving school was in a bakery, aged twelve, or as some accounts have it working for a year before this in the offices of the *Edinburgh Evening News*, where his elder brother Thomas also worked. Greaves accepts that Connolly did work at the *Evening News*, and that he started at the age of ten as a 'printer's devil'. This entailed running messages, making tea and generally being useful to the printers. He was sacked when his age was discovered by a factory inspector.

Parents were responsible by law for ensuring education in the three Rs, and John Connolly was a literate man, as shown by his confident signature on his marriage certificate. For a man of his background this was a little unusual and James might well have inherited a love of reading from his father; he refers later in life to his father setting him exercises.

Connolly's job at the bakery lasted about two years. The only reliable information on this period is what he later told his friend and mentor John Leslie. It appears that his health broke down under the strain and he then found work in a mosaic tiling depot in Frederick Street. He worked in the bakery until 1881 and left Edinburgh a year later, which means he spent only one year at the tile depot. There was no shortage of work in Edinburgh for young people during this time, but for working-class boys employment became harder to find the older and more costly they became, and they were quickly replaced by younger boys.

Connolly then decided to enlist in the British Army, as his eldest brother John had already done. But why did he opt for the British Army? He might have been simply following in John's footsteps, after reading his letters home extolling a life of adventure in India, where he was stationed. In any case, the younger brother adopted a false name and lied about his age when he enlisted, which was not an unusual practice at the time.

The army was not the only choice available to him, but it meant immediate escape from Cowgate, from Scotland and from dreary hard work. His daughter Nora recalls him telling her of his time working in the bakery: 'The few shillings I got were needed at home. Often I would pray fervently that I would find the place burnt down when I got there.'[3] The army might also have represented a chance to be trained in soldiering. The Fenian Brotherhood, the revolutionary organisation that planned the Rising, had a track record of infiltrating the British Army and using it so that young Nationalists would get first-class military training. This would involve stealing weapons, gathering information and so on. It is a tradition that survives to the present day, and I had experience of it during my involvement with the Provisional IRA.

Connolly later insisted that he joined the army solely for the purpose of training. In his book on Connolly, Donal Nevin produces a letter dated 29 April 1951 from John J. Lyng, acting secretary of the Irish Socialist Federation in New York, to William O'Brien, Connolly's colleague in Ireland. 'Here in the USA Irish Socialist clubroom Jim [Connolly] said of his military service: "I was carried away by the John Boyle O'Reilly propaganda to infiltrate the British army and found myself in India like most of the other Irishmen who enlisted for the same reason."'[4]* Connolly was born two years after O'Reilly was sentenced, but he would certainly have known about it and the reasons for it. This account, however, should be taken with a grain of salt since he almost certainly never served in India. The most logical

---

* O'Reilly had enlisted in the 10th Royal Hussars so that he could recruit Irishmen for the Fenians. He was sentenced to death in 1866 but this was commuted to life imprisonment and he was transported to Australia.

explanation is that he did not want his socialist comrades to know that he had served in Ireland.

Throughout the early 1880s the Land War dominated rural Ireland. Charles Stewart Parnell, Protestant land-owner and the leader of the Irish Parliamentary Party, described as the 'uncrowned King of Ireland', was the dominant figure of the era, uniting different strands of Nationalism in a quest for Home Rule and Land Reform. Connolly claims in his later writings to have been a militant Nationalist by this stage and to have devoured the literature of the Land League. His time in Ireland coincided with heightened agrarian tensions and violence between landlords and tenant farmers. It was a tough period in rural Ireland and the army frequently had to protect landowners from angry peasants and their violent secret societies, which were known by a variety of names such as Whiteboys, Moonlighters and Defenders.

Whatever his reasons, fourteen-year-old Connolly joined the King's Liverpool Regiment, the same unit as his brother. It was regarded as an Irish regiment; its uniform was green and its badge was a harp surmounted by a crown. Like most Irish regiments it had been targeted in the past for Fenian infiltration.

In July 1882 Connolly's battalion was sent to Cork, and it was there, in the uniform of the British Army, that he saw Ireland for the first time as a teenager and as a soldier. Desmond Greaves recounts that Connolly told a colleague called Mullery (or Mullary) about spending a night in Cork guarding a man called Joyce who had been found guilty of an agrarian outrage known as the Maamtrasna massacre, when five members of the same family were murdered. Joyce was hanged the following morning. We don't know if Connolly was present at the execution. According to Connolly and other accounts, the man was convicted on the flimsiest of evidence.

At my Christian Brothers primary school I recall hearing, from one teacher at least, that one of the great lies spread about Connolly was that he was not born in Ireland. He was also not a Marxist but a great Irish Nationalist Catholic patriot who had a special affinity with the poor. Kerry in the 1960s for those of my background was not big on questioning the martyr's narrative. To question was to be attacked as 'anti-national', a brutally effective tactic which succeeded all too well in stifling any debate or attempt at free thinking.

Connolly left the army before he had finished the seven-year service for which he had enlisted, and was therefore a deserter. After his execution, old friends in Edinburgh, wanting to protect his reputation, were more than happy to say that he was born in Ireland, that he came to Edinburgh with his family when he was about ten and then worked around Scotland from the age of fourteen, not returning to Edinburgh until he was twenty-one. Because he was a deserter, albeit a deserter with an assumed name, Connolly was also happy not to shed any light on this. According to Nevin, on 1 November 1916 John Leslie wrote that 'Connolly was away from Scotland for a considerable time and about this period of his life he was reticent... Understand me, I know the reason and to my mind, there was no occasion for reticence, but such was his wish.'[5]

Leslie may have been mistaken in this. Connolly himself sometimes wondered how he had managed to escape arrest as a deserter. One explanation is that by the time a count was taken when the regiment returned to England his seven years had elapsed and no one made very much of it. But in the light of his later activities, he was in no position to go around drawing attention to his service in the British Army. Jim Larkin, the Liverpool-born socialist and colleague of Connolly, also knew about his army background but chose never to refer to it either.

Not long before their wedding, Connolly, then living in Dundee, wrote to his fiancée telling her to meet him in Perth. Explaining that he was extremely poor, he then added: 'I could get plenty of work in England but England might be unhealthy for me, you understand.'[6] This shows that he might have been worried about being identified as a deserter. In later years he was known to say to close friends that he was surprised he was never challenged by the authorities.

The reasons for his desertion might well include that his battalion was to be sent to India and he'd just met the woman he wanted to marry. He had only months left to serve and perhaps he feared that if he was sent away he would have no choice but to serve out the battalion's posting there. Connolly could be extraordinarily impetuous and strong-willed; having made up his mind that he was going to marry he likely saw any impediment as a personal affront.

Looking at his later writings about the army it was evidently an institution he hated intensely. In the *Workers' Republic* in July 1899, he stated: 'The standing army in any country is a tool in the hands of the oppressor of the people and is a generator of prostitution: the British army is in this particular the most odious on the face of the earth.' In October that year, in the same publication, he wrote: 'The Army is, in plain matter-of-fact language, what the Socialists so blatantly describe it to be, viz. a body of hired assassins. The army is a veritable moral cesspool of corruption all within its bounds, and exuding forth a miasma of pestilence upon every spot so unfortunate to be cursed by its presence.'

Some years later, in 1915, also in the *Workers' Republic*, he went on to censor the way Irish women interacted socially with British soldiers in Dublin. In an article titled 'The Immorality of Dublin', he wrote: 'But if the reader will take his stand any night at the corner of O'Connell Street and Bachelor's Walk ... Or a dozen other places where people congregate he will see soldiers continually accosting and importuning girls and women and policemen smilingly looking on.' And later that year he continued the theme: 'Hence we have seen the spectacle of Irishmen posing as patriots actually petitioning the British government to establish military garrisons in their district. Willing that a foreign army may be in a position to coerce them, that their sons may be lured into its blood stained service and their daughters ruined by its lustful military.' As for the Irish wives and mothers of dead or injured soldiers, he was scathing, likening them to 'criminals waiting for the receipt of the blood money which the British government allows them in return for the limbs and lives of their husbands'.

While writing these articles (and there are many more in a similar vein), Connolly seems to have forgotten that his own wife, Lillie (née Reynolds), an Irish woman, met and fell in love with him, a British soldier, in Dublin in 1888.

Chapter 3

A SILENT YOUNG MAN TRANSFORMED

James Connolly met Lillie Reynolds in late 1887 or early 1888 when he was stationed in Beggars Bush army barracks in Dublin. They were both waiting for the same tram, which failed to stop, and they fell into conversation. Lillie was one of twins from Carnew in County Wicklow. Her father had died when she was very young, and she and her two brothers were raised by her mother. She was a year older than Connolly, and was working as a live-in domestic servant in Dublin when they met.

Lillie had been raised in the Church of Ireland, which conferred on her more of a formal education than was available to Connolly. When his time in the army was almost up they made plans. He would go to Aldershot to be demobbed and Lillie would go to London, where she had found employment. They intended to marry, but Connolly deserted and returned to Scotland, and although Lillie carried out her part and went to London and later to Perth, there followed delay and confusion for their marriage plans.

During this period they wrote to each other frequently. Donal Nevin publishes six of Connolly's letters, which are held in William O'Brien's papers in the National Library of Ireland. The letters make clear that Connolly was near destitute in Scotland and Lillie was helping him out financially. He writes with a mixture of gratitude and self-pity. An extract from a letter written just before their marriage clarifies where Connolly's priorities lay, and how they would dominate Lillie's life. The letter concludes:

> By the way if we get married next week I shall be unable to go to Dundee as I promised, as my fellow-workmen in the job are preparing for a strike on the end of this month, for a reduction in the hours of labour. As my brother and I are ringleaders in the matter it is necessary we should be on the ground. If we were not we should be looked upon as blacklegs, which the Lord forbid. Mind don't lose a minutes time in writing, and you will greatly gratify.
>
> Your loving Jim (Not James as your last letter was directed.)[1]

There can be no doubt that Lillie Reynolds must have known the kind of man she was marrying, though she might not have foreseen the hardships she would endure over the next twenty-six years. Following her husband's execution she was forced to navigate her way through the Ireland of the 1920s and 30s alone and be there for her six children.

Connolly stayed in Dundee for most of 1888, and it was here that he first became openly involved in socialist and labour agitation. His brother John was also based there, and was active in the Social Democratic Federation, whose most prominent member was John Leslie. Leslie eventually became Connolly's mentor and played a major role in his life before Connolly returned to Ireland, a return that was greatly facilitated by Leslie's personal intervention.

When Connolly arrived in Dundee it was a hive of socialist activity, with the Social Democratic Federation and the Socialist League leading the way. Strikes, protests and public meetings were commonplace and often drew large crowds. Leslie spoke at a public meeting in Dundee on 1 April, and it seems likely this was when they first met and where Connolly was inducted into the SDF.

Writing twenty-five years later, Leslie recalls his first encounter with Connolly: 'I noticed the silent young man as a very interested and constant attendant at the open air meetings. Once when a sustained and virulent personal attack was being made upon myself and when I was almost succumbing to it, Connolly sprung upon the stool, and to say the least of it, retrieved the situation. I never forgot it. The following week, he joined our organisation, and it is needless to say what an acquisition he was.'[2]

That Connolly was a brilliant orator was also confirmed by Darrell Figgis in his eye-witness account of the 1916 Rising. Describing him as 'of middle height sturdy of frame and broad of brow he suggested and his Northern accent conveyed, the thought of a realist who lived to slay illusions … He would sit, a lifeless heap, the picture of gloom, until it came his time to speak, then with three strides he would throw off his gloom like a cloak and pour out eloquence like molten metal that scorched and burned all before it.'[3]

Before James and Lillie could get married they had to obtain a dispensation from the Bishop of Dunkeld in Perth, which meant that Lillie had to meet with the priest who would marry them and reside in Perth for three weeks before the wedding. In a letter Connolly wrote to Lillie dated 6 April 1890 he stated: 'You know before a Catholic can marry a Protestant he must obtain what is called a dispensation from the Bishop. I have applied for this dispensation, and I am informed it can only be granted on condition that you promise never to interfere with my observance of my religion (funny idea, isn't it) and that any children of the union should have to be baptised in the Catholic Church.'[4] The sarcastic aside 'funny idea, isn't it' shows what Connolly thought even then of his religious observance.

He and Lillie were married in Perth in the spring of 1890 and set up home in Edinburgh, near to Cowgate. Immediately Connolly threw himself into socialist agitation in his home town. His eldest brother, John, was now working full time as a carter for Edinburgh Council, and soon after his marriage Connolly found casual employment there.

At this time Edinburgh, not Glasgow, was the centre of socialist thought and agitation, something that Connolly appeared to struggle with. Glasgow had a greater concentration of industrialised working class, but this apparent dichotomy can be partly explained by the fact that Edinburgh University was a haven for political refugees. The city contained a quality of socialist thought and leadership not found elsewhere in Scotland during this period. Yet socialism was most attractive to unskilled workers, many of whom were Irish, and a large percentage of them had been active in the Land League. Connolly took full advantage of the opportunity to observe and learn.

During this period Connolly met and worked with Leo Meillet, a French refugee and former mayor of a Paris commune. At a meeting in Edinburgh in 1889 to commemorate the 1871 Paris Commune, Meillet said that without the shedding of blood there could be no social salvation.* Later, in Dublin, Connolly would organise an annual commemoration of the Paris Commune.

The Scottish Socialist Federation, with which John Leslie was prominently involved, ran a series of study

---

* Reading this statement now, even though once I would have heartily agreed with it, the cold, casual brutality fills me with horror.

groups, and it was here that Connolly acquired a grounding in socialist literature – including Marx's *Das Kapital*, *The Communist Manifesto* and writings by Friedrich Engels and William Morris – as he began to apply Marxist principles to his rather incoherent socialist and Nationalist beliefs.

In 1893, aged twenty-four, Connolly joined the Independent Labour Party, which had just been established by Keir Hardie. Later that year he became secretary of the Edinburgh branch of the Scottish Socialist Federation, of which John Leslie had previously been secretary. The organ of the Federation was called *Justice*, and it was in this paper that Connolly's first published work appeared, on 18 January 1893.

Although these first pieces are little more than records of the activities of the branch, his trenchant and vigorous prose style can be clearly seen in a response to a suggestion that the Federation set up a branch in Leith, the industrial area outside Edinburgh. The capital city, Connolly wrote, was largely composed of 'snobs, flunkeys, mashers, lawyers, students, middle-class pensioners and dividend hunters'. Working-class Leith, on the other hand, had its 'due proportion of sweaters, slave-drivers, rack-renting slum landlords, shipping-federation agents, and parasites of every description'. For these reasons, Leith might 'have been reasonably expected to develop socialistic principles more readily than the Modern Athens'.[5]

Barely able to support his family with his part-time

work as a carter for Edinburgh Council, Connolly was by now the father of two children: Mona was born in 1891 and Nora in 1893. There was also some intermittent financial support from the Scottish Socialist Federation.

The years 1890–4 were a period of learning for Connolly, during which he acquired a sure grasp of Marxist theory, developed his writing skills and learned how to organise and agitate, while continuing to be deeply influenced by John Leslie's Marxist analysis of Irish history.

In the winter of 1893 Leslie delivered a series of lectures to the Scottish Socialist Federation in Edinburgh, which Connolly attended. Centred on why Leslie believed that the Land League had been sold out by the Home Rule movement, during these lectures Leslie hammered out a new line of thought. Beginning in March 1894, he published his 'Passing Thoughts on the Irish Question', which were subsequently collected and issued as a pamphlet called *The Present Position of the Irish Question.*

Leslie blamed the Kilmainham Treaty and Parnell for agreeing to subvert the agrarian movement in return for the release of political prisoners. He saw the Land League as a truly revolutionary organisation, and the Home Rule movement as composed of 'large landowners, prosperous businessmen, and journalists, blatant and bigoted self-constituted champions of the Catholic Faith, with only a small sprinkling of really earnest and sincere, if somewhat narrow-minded nationalists'.[6] According to him, the Land League had fought a hard and bitter struggle for two years, its leaders had been imprisoned and the League declared an illegal association. The Kilmainham Treaty was a 'sell out', although he retained a degree of affection for Parnell: 'The gloomy and tragic close of his great and stormy life, his death, the death of a Titan strangled by pigmies, which wrung tears from those who never forgave him his actions in the manner of the Kilmainham Treaty.'[7]

With those words Leslie also showed himself to be a man of humanity and forgiveness; qualities which his pupil James Connolly never absorbed. Leslie was too rounded an individual to indulge in the personal and ideological feuds that Connolly thrived on.

In November 1894 Connolly contested the municipal elections for the St Giles ward in Edinburgh. He was selected as a candidate for the Scottish Socialist Federation, but to preserve unity within the diverse factions he was put forward as an independent socialist candidate. He did quite well in the election, coming in third with 14 per cent of the poll. Perhaps the sweetest part of it for Connolly and the socialists was their defeat of the candidate standing as an 'Irishman and a Catholic', who got a meagre fifty-four votes.

By late 1895 Connolly and his family were in dire straits. It was a particularly hard winter in Scotland and work was difficult to find with so many unemployed all searching for scraps. Connolly had been getting casual work as a carter, with a private contractor to the Council, but he appears either to have been fired or the work dried up. He was also devoting most of his energies to his socialist agitation and was now writing regularly in several periodicals, none of which provided anything like enough money to support a wife and two young children.

So Connolly set off on a great new adventure to earn a living: he decided to open a cobbler's shop. He advertised his services in the socialist papers, but soon found that even socialists wanted a decent service and good shoes. He was far too wrapped up in politics to give the new business the attention it needed.

The fact that he was also a useless cobbler was witnessed by schoolgirl Anna Munro, who was later to become a suffragette, and whose family was sympathetic to Connolly. Having decided to help out by bringing all the family footwear to him for repair, she later recalled that not a shoe or a boot could ever be worn again. The business venture quickly folded, and Connolly remarked that he was going out to buy a mirror to watch himself starve to death. Some people say that Connolly bore his poverty with great dignity. It might be truer to say that his family, with little choice, bore the brunt of his 'dignity'.

He believed that his political activities made him unemployable and he set out to get more paid work within the socialist movement, to which he was devoting an increasing amount of his time. It is also clear that this was the only work that interested him. He was a born activist who needed a cause bigger than himself, bigger than his family – a cause he could dedicate everything to, and sacrifice everything for, including his life and his loved ones. He was becoming a true believer of the extreme kind, a man who was destined for martyrdom.

And so he began to advertise for work as a speaker and organiser, but it appears there was no response. An article in *Justice* on 22 June 1895 stated that Connolly found it impossible to get employment in his native town, and that he was a martyr whose martyrdom would have been saved if certain men had been honourable enough to fulfil their obligations to him. It is not known what these obligations were or who had entered them, but it may have been linked to the failure of the cobbler's shop. There is evidence, even at this stage, that Connolly's generally high-handed attitude to his comrades did not always produce the results he wanted. At around this time he was sharply reprimanded during an internal row over election material that he had sent to the printer without first clearing it with the local organisation.

Beset by problems from all sides, Connolly began to discuss the notion of emigrating. He discovered that the government of Chile was offering passage and a grant of land and tools, though there is no real evidence to suggest that this should be taken seriously. When he told Leslie he was thinking of emigrating, probably in a fit of pique, Leslie decided to make a personal appeal on Connolly's behalf in *Justice* on 14 December 1895. 'Here is a man among men,' Leslie wrote. 'I am not much given to flattery, as those who know me are aware, yet I may say that very few men have I met deserving of greater love and respect than James Connolly.' He went on to describe him as 'the most able propagandist in every sense of the word that Scotland has turned out'. Unable to resist a dig at Edinburgh activists, Leslie continued: 'Leaving the Edinburgh Socialists to digest the matter, is there no comrade in Glasgow, Dundee or anywhere else who could secure a situation for one of the most self-sacrificing men in the movement?'[8]

There was no interest in Scotland but the appeal was answered from Dublin. The Dublin Socialist Club offered Connolly a job as organiser on a salary of £1 a week, which he accepted. And so, as a direct result of Leslie's intervention, Connolly's immediate circumstances and those of his family changed. It was a decision that would have profound implications for them, as well as for Ireland.

Connolly must have been happy at the prospect of full-time work as a socialist organiser, and perhaps Lillie was happy to move; she, after all, was going home. Two months before they left Scotland, Aideen, their third daughter, was born, the first in their family to be given an Irish name. Lillie was moving back to her country of birth, where she had lived, worked and played for twenty-two years. Her husband, however, was going back to a place he knew only from his army days, and which, judging by the scraps of recollection available and what he later wrote about the army, he seems not to have overly enjoyed.

The family arrived in Dublin in May 1896 and found

accommodation in a room in Charlemont in the inner city. Before May was out, Connolly had imposed his will on the Dublin Socialist Club, which soon broke apart to be replaced by an organisation – the Irish Socialist Republican Party – exactly reflecting his own beliefs.

The first meeting of the ISRP took place in the snug of a pub in Dublin on 29 May 1896, and the public statement he made on behalf of the new party summed up exactly where he now was in terms of his political beliefs and theories. It also looked ahead to what eventually led him to take part in the 1916 Rising. 'The struggle for Irish freedom has two aspects; it is national and it is social,' he declared. 'The national ideal can never be realised until Ireland stands forth before the world as a nation, free and independent. It is social and economic because no matter what the form of government may be, as long as one class owns as private property the land and instruments of labour from which mankind derive their substance, that class will always have it in their power to plunder and enslave the remainder of their fellow creatures.'[9]

There is no sense here that Connolly was an advocate of violent or armed struggle; indeed, most socialists and trade unionists of the period believed that progress to socialism should or would come in the context of co-operation within the union of Ireland and Great Britain. But, crucially, he was arguing that an Irish Republic was a prerequisite to the establishment of socialism, a path that would later open the door to his alliance with militant Nationalists.

For Connolly's wife and family these years in Dublin were dominated by extreme poverty, with only occasional labouring work providing some respite. Neither did Connolly's political career go smoothly. At one public meeting he was loudly heckled amid a shower of missiles. 'You're not an Irishman,' someone shouted.

In 1897 he met Maud Gonne, a fabled beauty and passion of W.B. Yeats. She was also a romantic and somewhat histrionic Irish Nationalist, and they formed a bond that survived until Connolly's death. They co-operated in a series of demonstrations during the celebrations of Queen Victoria's Diamond Jubilee, during which an elderly woman was killed and the ensuing protests gained a great deal of press coverage. Connolly was briefly imprisoned until Gonne paid his fine.

The centenary of the 1798 rebellion was the occasion for much commemoration in Ireland and amnesty committees were formed to press for the release of Fenian prisoners in jail in England. While most Nationalists did not support the violent actions of the Fenians, agitating for the release of prisoners, once a respectable time has passed, has long been a relatively popular activity in Nationalist Ireland, and many of the people who took part in the Easter Rising cited this period as influential, in some cases pivotal, to their involvement. Organisations that were involved included the Gaelic League, the Gaelic Athletic Association, the Irish Parliamentary Party and, as ever, the Irish Republican Brotherhood. 'From trade unions to abstinence associations, there were few societies that Fenians would not subvert in an effort "to instill patriotism in its members".'[10]

Connolly and the ISRP were engaged in a similar exercise, but their influence was limited. Having largely failed to use the Diamond Jubilee celebrations to introduce socialism to Nationalist politics, he decided to establish the *Workers' Republic*, which was launched on 13 August 1898, Connolly having secured a loan of £50 from Keir Hardie.

In 1899 Connolly organised protests against the Boer War, but the public response was poor. Sean O'Casey describes watching Connolly and Maud Gonne in a commandeered brake during a protest in Dublin. In *Pictures in the Hallway* he wrote: 'A long car, benched on both sides, drawn by two frightened hearse horses. A stout, short, stocky man, whose face was hidden by a wide-awake hat, was driving them. Several other men, pale-faced and tight lipped, sat on the seats facing each other, and with them was a young woman with long lovely yellow hair, smiling happily, like a child out on her first excursion.'[11]

Connolly was remarkably tolerant of upper-class women like Maud Gonne and Constance Markievicz, perhaps because they both appeared to idolise him, and also because they had instrumentality – money, transport, accommodation and status – all of which he so singularly lacked. The two women were of different political persuasions: Gonne was a right-wing Nationalist and Markievicz, a left-wing radical (who would take part in the Rising with Connolly's Irish Citizen Army), was imprisoned several times and later became an MP. In the years before the Rising, Connolly stayed mostly at her house, a haven for extreme Nationalists and socialists and young boys from Na Fianna Eireann, the Nationalist Boy Scout movement she had helped to found.

In November 1897 the ISRP published a pamphlet titled *Erin's Hope: The End and the Means.* This was a collection of six articles by Connolly, three of them already published in *Labour Weekly*, the paper of Keir Hardie's Independent Labour Party. The other three had been published in the *Shan Van Vocht*, a monthly magazine founded by Alice Milligan in Belfast in 1896, which came under the influence of the Irish Republican Brotherhood. Students and biographers of Connolly regard this as a significant moment in his development as a writer and thinker. It was Connolly's first major exposition of his views on the Irish question and summed up lucidly his understanding of the issues facing the working classes, politically and socially. In my view, and in many others', the basis for virtually all of his subsequent writings can be found in this pamphlet.

Reading it today I am struck by how Connolly reduces the complex problem of Anglo-Irish relations to one of fundamentally different systems of land ownership. He maintained that 'common ownership of land formed the basis of primitive society in almost every country but that, exceptionally in Ireland, primitive communism as a system formed part of a well-defined social organisation up to the seventeenth century.' The rival systems of land ownership was 'the pivot around which centred all the struggles and rebellions of which Irish history has been so prolific'. He also wrote that 'the days of small farmers, like small capitalists are gone', and he derided 'industrialization in Ireland as impossible because it lacked resources for investment and a market for manufactured goods'.[12] Much of this was a serious attempt to provide a Marxist alternative to the standard 'kings and queens' story of Irish history, and it was a new and fresh approach. However, without title to private property, freedom and society as we know it today simply would not exist. In truth, 'primitive communism' never moved beyond primitive clan ownership and the clan leader was the boss. As soon as Irish peasants won the right to own their land they would kill rather than hand it over to communal ownership.

More relevant and important for me and many other young men and women in Ireland was Connolly's ringing declaration in the same pamphlet: 'If you remove the English army tomorrow and hoist the green flag over Dublin Castle, unless you set about the organisation of the Socialist Republic your efforts would be in vain. England would still rule you.' These two sentences are among the most recognised and quoted of Connolly's words. Today they introduce one to the Eirigi website, a dissident Republican socialist party, several of whose members have been arrested and are serving prison sentences for terrorist offences.

In early 1901 Connolly sought speaking engagements in Great Britain. The previous Christmas the Irish Socialist Republican Party had provided him with a week's wage of just two shillings. The Connolly family's prospects were bleak, especially as Lillie had recently given birth to their sixth child. Having received a positive response from Scotland, he spoke that summer in Aberdeen, Glasgow, Falkirk and Leith.

This brought him to the attention of the Socialist Labor Party of America, and in particular to its charismatic leader, Daniel De Leon, who helped out the ISRP financially. De Leon was an uncompromising Marxist who believed that a socialist party should be as 'intolerant as science'. For a while Connolly fell strongly under his influence and was soon invited to America. In August of 1902 he set sail for a three-month speaking tour during which he addressed mainly Irish-American audiences. It was to be his first American experience, but certainly not his last.

On his return to Ireland he was soon involved in internal rows with the ISRP. These had begun while he was in America, where he wrote several angry letters complaining about their lack of commitment and how the organisation was being managed. The details of these rows are not important, but on one occasion when he was back in Ireland, Connolly offered to resign, and much to his surprise it was accepted.

Another biographer of Connolly, Samuel Levenson, had no doubt that much of the blame for the ISRP's collapse must 'certainly be attributed to Connolly's own personality'. He goes on to write that 'he was unable to understand the feelings of those who did not share his convictions. He was even more impatient with those who shared his feelings but did not act twenty-four hours a day upon them.'[13] Anyone who has spent any time in a revolutionary organisation will be familiar with this type of fanaticism. Of this period Greaves also noted that Connolly was capable of moods of deep depression, a reaction perhaps to his punishing workload.

Connolly's eyes soon strayed once again towards America. There were a number of reasons for this. The ISRP was virtually dead, the *Workers' Republic* had ceased publication and his large family was reduced to extreme poverty because of his single-minded pursuit of his vision. America was also where the action was. There was as yet no Marxist country in the world, no workers' republic anywhere, and Connolly, like many European and American Marxists of the period, including De Leon, believed that America would fulfil the prophecy of Marx, and bring the downfall of capitalism the world over.

Connolly left Ireland an extremely bitter man. In a letter to William O'Brien, he wrote: 'As you say the conditions under which I existed in Ireland were very hard to my family and myself, but hard as they were, they were not hard enough to drive me from the country.' It is an extraordinary letter in which he pours vitriol on his former comrades in the ISRP. He writes that 'these things [the arguments] have changed the whole course of my life, but my conscience is clear, as my judgement was correct; let those who are responsible for those acts be assured that no amount of belated praise can gild the pill or sweeten the bitterness of my exile.' He finishes with these lines: 'My career has been unique in many things. In this last, it is so also. Men have been driven out of Ireland by the British Government and by the landlords, but I am the first driven out by the Socialists.'[14]

Connolly was thirty-five when he set sail for America on 18 September 1903, leaving his wife and children, who were to join him once he had settled in. After seven years of work as a socialist organiser in Ireland, not one socialist came to see him off. Samuel Levenson describes it as 'a graphic illustration of his isolation and defeat'. It is unlikely that De Leon was overjoyed by Connolly's desire to go back to America. As far as he was concerned, Connolly was a disciple who had been brought to America primarily to be indoctrinated. He felt he was useful with Irish-Americans, but he was far from a major player. Reading De Leon's comments now, it is pretty clear that at times he felt Connolly to be no more than an irritant.

That was not how Connolly saw himself, however. Almost from the moment he landed in America he was ready to challenge De Leon on points of Marxist doctrine. Did Connolly see himself as the man to lead the socialist revolution in America, or at least play a pivotal role?

Suffice to say that he considered himself the equal of any man, no matter the objective reality. Once in America, he had hoped to be employed as a printer by the *Weekly People*, the paper of the Socialist Labor Party, but this did not happen, leaving him angry with the Party, its paper and De Leon, who was the editor. The actuality was that Connolly did not have a union card and without this it was almost impossible to get work in the printing industry.

After a couple of weeks in New York he moved to Troy, a small city upstate. Here he lived with his cousins Helen and Thomas Humes at 447 Tenth Street. He found work with the Metropolitan Life Insurance Company and joined the local branch of the Socialist Labor Party. He almost immediately initiated a serious row with De Leon, the first of many in what was to be seven years in America. The first row was about whether or not workers should struggle for higher wages in the advance towards socialism. De Leon held that this was pointless and was opposed, claiming that prices always rose with wages. Connolly's disagreement was based on Marx's theory of value, price and profit and how this applied in the workers' daily struggle. Their dispute played out in the Party's newspaper.

The most interesting part of all this is the insight it gives into Connolly's state of mind at the time. Whatever the truth of these interminable rows, he and his family were about to suffer another great blow. After living in America for almost a year he was ready for Lillie and the children to join him in Troy. But just before their departure his eldest daughter, thirteen-year-old Mona, set her clothes on fire while lifting a pot from a stove in her aunt's house. Badly burned, she died in hospital the following day.

The RMS *Cedric* docked at Ellis Island on 14 August 1904; on board were Lillie Connolly and her five surviving children. Their names and ages are listed in the manifest and passenger record as: Nora (10), Aideen (8), Ina (6), Moira (4) and Roderick (3). Heartbreakingly, the record also included Mona (13). Connolly and his wife submitted a note to the *Weekly People* thanking everyone who had commiserated with them on Mona's death.

That November, three months after the arrival of his family, Connolly lost his job. He went to New York, where he stayed with Jack Mulray, an old friend from ISRP days, while he found temporary employment with another insurance company. He did not return to his family in Troy until April 1905, when he obtained a position as the local representative of the Pacific Mutual Life Insurance Company. Soon after this, however, there was a strike against conditions in nine shirt and collar factories in Troy. The strike lasted fourteen weeks and Connolly spent more time collecting for the strikers than for his company, and he lost this job too.

Writing, speaking and working on behalf of the Party occupied Connolly's life until the founding of the Industrial Workers of the World union in Chicago in 1905. This was important for Connolly because the

Wobblies, as they came to be known, transformed the socialist scene in America. Connolly embraced Industrial Unionism, which became better known in Europe as Syndicalism or the 'One Big Union', and believed that the Industrial Workers of the World would absorb both the Socialist Labor Party and the Socialist Party of America before sweeping to power.

There followed more interminable rows between Connolly and De Leon, perhaps best summed up by the American historian James Stevenson in *Clashing Personalities*: 'Virtually powerless to bring about the great social transformation which they so ardently desired, they [De Leon and Connolly] fluctuated between despair and unrealistic expectations ... and James Connolly was not quite so tall a man that he could not stoop to attack a political ally for purely personal reasons.' Both men, wrote Stevenson, 'allowed their personal spite, anger, jealousy and bitterness to undermine their common principle and strategy'.[15] Their turbulent relationship came to an end in September 1908 when Connolly joined the Socialist Party of America and De Leon was kicked out of the Industrial Workers of the World.

In February 1907 Connolly formed the Irish Socialist Federation, which published a journal called *The Harp*. The first issue appeared in January 1908 and was mostly written by Connolly himself. The Irish Socialist Federation never had more than a handful of members and the circulation of *The Harp* never more than 2,000. In her autobiography, *I Speak My Own Piece*, the labour activist

Elizabeth Gurley Flynn wrote: 'It was a pathetic sight to see him [Connolly] standing, poorly clad, at the door of Cooper Union or some other East Side Hall, selling his little paper.' Gurley Flynn was the American-born daughter of Irish immigrants, who Connolly first met when she was seventeen. 'He was short, rather stout, a plain looking man,' she recalled, 'with large black moustaches, a very high forehead and dark sad eyes, a man who rarely smiled.'[16]

Frank Bohn, a comrade of Connolly's in America, recalled visiting him at home in 1908, when Connolly was compiling his pamphlet, *Socialism Made Easy*. The purpose of his visit was to persuade Connolly to mend his fences with De Leon. Writing in the *New York Post* just after Connolly's execution he wrote:

'I found him sick in bed surrounded by his wife and six small children [the eldest was under fourteen]. They were actually suffering from lack of food and the rent was overdue. The white face of Connolly lay back on the pillow and his voice was weak. Sick as he was, Connolly was busy on *Socialism Made Easy*. "I shall never make peace with that man!" Connolly said. "He has his paper [*the People*] and I have no means of redress, but he is wrong and I am right."'[17]

Any examination of Connolly's time in America would be incomplete without mentioning that it was here that he wrote most of his *Labour in Irish History*, which was published in Ireland on his return in 1910. Widely regarded as his magnum opus, it established him as a serious socialist thinker and writer. I read it in fits and starts over a number of years, but like many others in Ireland – though I suspect they might not like to admit it – I found it heavy going. Many socialists and Republicans claim it was a huge influence in their political development, but for me it lacked perspective and succeeded in being both overly dogmatic and sentimental. Even as a young man I used to wonder how could the richness and variety of human life be made subservient to such a rigid, overarching ideology?

In 1909 the prominent Republican Helena Moloney wrote to Connolly from Dublin, deploring the threatened suspension of *The Harp*, saying: 'I only wish it was in Ireland that you were publishing the paper.' This mirrored Connolly's own thoughts, and by now he wanted out of America. At around this time other comrades also wrote to him, encouraging him to come back to Ireland.

A little later that year he wrote to his old comrade, John Carstairs Matheson:* 'Well, you people are all contributing to make me homesick. I wrote to my Dublin comrades saying I had all the will and desire in the world to get home out of this cursed country but I can't. The District Council owes me eighty dollars back salary. I am now off the payroll and the misery and hunger in New

---

* Matheson and Connolly were comrades from the early days of Connolly's socialist activities in Scotland. Matheson was one of the few constants in his life and they regularly exchanged letters over many years.

York are dreadful. I am simply frightened at the immediate outlook for my family and myself. How then to get
home?'[18]

In another letter, to William O'Brien, his comrade from
ISRP days in Ireland, Connolly wrote: 'I am not satisfied
here, have not near the enthusiasm for the fight that I
had in Ireland and want to get among people with whom
I feel I have more in common.' In June 1905 he had
written to Jack Mulray musing over a possible return to
Ireland, but finishing with the words: 'I regard Ireland,
or at least the Socialist part of Ireland which is all I care
for, as having thrown me out, and I do not wish to return
like a dog to his vomit.'[19] He was evidently still bitter
about what had happened with the ISRP. By now he
was an organiser for the Socialist Party of America, a
reasonably paid job, yet he wrote to Matheson: 'I feel that
most anyone can do the work I am doing here but that
there is work to be done in Ireland I can do better than
most anyone.'

Connolly's final involvement with the struggle for
American workers came during strikes by steel workers
in Pittsburgh in 1909. He had visited the area several
times on behalf of the Socialist Party of America and
had condemned the conditions they were forced to
endure. In a letter to the *Pittsburgh Leader* newspaper
on 15 July 1909, Father Toner, pastor of St Mary's Catholic
Church, wrote: 'A man is given less consideration than
a dog and dead bodies are simply kicked aside while
the men are literally driven to their death.' After a vicious

struggle, the eventual settlement complied with nearly all the strikers' demands.

Unlike when he had left Ireland, Connolly was given a warm send-off from America with a dinner at Cavanaugh's restaurant in New York, which was attended by prominent American socialists. Rows with De Leon and others notwithstanding, he was without doubt regarded as having made a significant contribution to the American labour movement, and there are statues commemorating this contribution in Troy and Chicago.

During his time in America he had been involved in and witnessed some very ugly and violent industrial disputes. Strikers and hired agents of employers often fought pitched battles where the use of guns and other weapons were not uncommon. Yet he had made a life for himself and his family and, almost for the first time, was beginning to be rewarded for his efforts. Having fallen out with almost every socialist in Ireland, it now seemed he could not wait to get back.

Chapter 4

MOBILISATION

Connolly landed in Derry on Monday 25 July 1910, once again without his family, and went to Dublin the following day. He immediately visited the fiery, Liverpool-born socialist Jim Larkin, who was imprisoned in Mountjoy jail. Larkin was by now the best-known Marxist agitator in the country. Of Irish parentage, he had moved to Dublin, where in 1909 he founded the Irish Transport and General Workers Union. A charismatic figure and a powerful orator, he was also ill-disciplined and difficult to work with. In many respects he was the Arthur Scargill of his day.

In his first year back in Ireland Connolly threw himself into the work of organising the Socialist Party of Ireland, speaking, writing and setting up new branches in Belfast, Dublin and Cork. But in reality the popularity of socialism in Ireland had hardly improved from when the ISRP was formed, and Connolly still found it difficult to earn a living. There was much toing and froing among William O'Brien, Connolly and Larkin about a position and salary for Connolly, but nothing was really decided and soon he began to talk about leaving Ireland again.

His family made it back from America in early December 1910. According to his daughter Ina, her mother was as reluctant to return to Ireland as she had been to go to America.[1] It was in America that Lillie had made a stable home, even if her husband was seldom there. As always with Connolly, his cause was everything. A relentless pattern had been established: Lillie would create a home, and her husband would destroy it under the remorseless lash of his ego. There was also a new addition to the family: baby Mona, now aged three.

Nora was now eighteen, and unable to find work in Dublin she moved to Belfast, where she found a job in a sweatshop. In May 1911 the family followed her there. Ina worked in a laundry and later joined Nora in the sweatshop, sewing aprons on a piecework basis. Once in Belfast, Connolly took on the role of Ulster organiser for the Irish Transport and General Workers Union, which had no more than a nominal existence there.

Soon he was behaving as expected: writing, organising strikes, recruiting for the union and falling out with other union officials. It was also his first experience of Belfast's sectarianism, and it left a strong impression. Religious and ethnic division had almost completely ruled out any serious possibility of working-class unity. Unlike most of

Ireland, Belfast was overwhelmingly a product of the Industrial Revolution. It was also largely Unionist in outlook, which meant the majority of its industrial workers were Protestant and favoured retaining the union between Great Britain and Ireland, and belonged to British trade unions. An avowed Republican socialist like Connolly was always going to have difficulty making headway there.

The long, drawn-out battle at Westminster for Irish Home Rule – involving a cast including Disraeli, Gladstone, Parnell, Isaac Butt, John Redmond, Lord Salisbury and a host of British and Irish parliamentarians – took a decisive turn when, after the 1910 general election, the Irish Parliamentary Party held the balance of power at Westminster. The big question was: how strong would Unionist resistance be in Ulster, and what form would it take?

In April 1912 Herbert Asquith, as prime minister, introduced the Third Home Rule Bill, a modest measure of self-government, which satisfied most Irish Nationalists who saw their future within the Empire. It involved the creation of a devolved Irish parliament, with responsibility for most internal matters, an appointed senate and an elected lower house within the framework of the United Kingdom of Great Britain and Ireland. In Belfast Connolly attacked the Bill, demanding it include proportional representation, women's suffrage, and that the proposal for an upper house be dropped. He was not an advocate of Home Rule; he wanted a full-blown, 32-county Irish

Republic, and was aggressively opposed to any opt-out clause for Unionists in Ulster. But, significantly, he did not attack the substance of the Home Rule Bill, even though he regarded it as nothing more than a staging post to an Irish Worker's Republic.

Connolly was often a lonely fighter for women's rights and is generally lauded for being ahead of his time in this regard. In the early 1970s John Lennon and Yoko Ono co-wrote the song 'Woman Is the Nigger of the World'. Amid much controversy over the title, Lennon said on American TV that the song was inspired by the Irish revolutionary James Connolly. To my mind, it is no more than a statement of the obvious to say that the poverty and suffering Connolly's wife and children had to endure, as well as their complete sublimation to his ambitions, suggests that, domestically at least, Connolly was guilty of hypocrisy.

In September 1912 on Ulster Day, almost a quarter of a million Ulster Unionists signed the Solemn League and Covenant dedicating them 'to defeat the present conspiracy to set up Home Rule in Ireland'. Connolly was the only future leader of the 1916 Rising resident in Belfast at this time, and he treated Unionists' concerns with overt contempt. During one of his open-air lectures in Belfast he was interrupted by a Unionist brandishing a copy of the Solemn League and Covenant. The man exclaimed that Unionists would see to it that there would be no Home Rule. Connolly told him to take the document home and frame it, adding, 'Your children will laugh at it.' Well, they did not laugh, and neither have their children's children.

In January 1913 the Third Reading of the Home Rule Bill was carried by a majority of over 100 in Parliament. By the end of that month the Ulster Volunteer Force was formed and Unionists were signalling their intent to break from the rest of Ireland when the Bill came into force, which now seemed certain. In September Unionist leader Sir Edward Carson announced that a provisional government for Ulster was ready to take control once Home Rule came into effect.

From 1910 Connolly had believed that a Home Rule parliament would be established, and focused much of his efforts on the need to form an Irish Labour Party that would ensure a socialist presence in the new administration. Although ferociously opposed to partition and prepared to resist it by any means, he knew a government concession to Ulster Unionists was the likely outcome of the British parliamentary process and that it would be accepted by most Nationalists, at least as a temporary measure. He was scathingly dismissive of the threats of violence from Ulster Unionists and simply thought they were bluffing.

With the support of Larkin and O'Brien, Connolly went ahead with his plan to establish an Irish Labour Party. In May 1912 the Irish Trades Union Congress met in Clonmel, County Tipperary, and Connolly, on behalf of the Belfast branch of the Irish Transport and General Workers Union, proposed that an Irish Labour Party be formed. The resolution was passed by forty-nine votes to eighteen. There is therefore no doubt that Connolly was a principal founder of the Party and is commonly accepted as the inspiration behind its formation. The British Labour Party, which normally organised in Ireland, ceded to the Irish Labour Party in 1913. This was rejected by many anti-Home Rule trade unionists in Belfast (the vast majority) and they formed the Belfast Labour Party, later to become the Northern Ireland Labour Party.

Then, on 29 August 1913, Connolly received a telegram from Larkin. He was immediately to leave for Dublin, where all-out war had broken out between workers and employers. Connolly packed his bags and headed off once again, leaving his family in Belfast. Larkin was riding high. His union, the Irish Transport and General Workers Union, controlled much of the unskilled labour in Dublin. He felt ready to take on the city's most powerful employer, William Martin Murphy, who he lambasted in word and print as a 'blood sucking vampire'.*

What had happened was this: when Larkin began to organise the workers at the Murphy-owned Dublin United Tramways Company, Murphy refused to recognise the union and dismissed Larkin's followers from his company. He also dismissed members of the union from the *Irish Independent*, which he also owned. On 26 August, 700 tram-workers went on strike, and three days later

* Murphy was a Home Rule-supporting, Irish Catholic businessman.

Murphy made his move to smash Larkin. First, he called a meeting of the Employers Federation Ltd, and after further meetings 400 employers voted to lock out all employees who were members of the ITGWU.

Connolly arrived in Dublin and was arrested the following day, 30 August. A public meeting was held and serious rioting followed in which over 400 people were injured. Two men were to die in further trouble that weekend. By the end of September at least 25,000 men were out of work, and as many as 100,000 faced hunger and deprivation.

After a week-long hunger strike, Connolly was released from jail on 14 September. He was one of the first Irish political hunger strikers, a tactic he borrowed from British suffragettes. On his release he took charge of the ITGWU while Larkin was in Britain canvassing aid from Labour supporters. Money was duly raised, and food ships began to arrive in Dublin by late September of that year.

Connolly then travelled to Scotland briefly to raise support, but when he arrived back in Dublin he found that Larkin had been imprisoned for seven months. All responsibility for the protest was now his. Larkin had given his blessing to a plan to have the strikers' children taken to England to be looked after. The Irish Catholic Church response was instant and savage. Priests picketed boats to England, and Archbishop Walsh condemned 'worthless mothers who would send their children to a strange land without security of any kind that those the poor children are to be handed over to are Catholics'.[2]

It was a tactical mistake, all too typical of Larkin, and Connolly set about sorting it out. He cancelled the plan, and then suspended free meals at Liberty Hall, head-quarters of the ITGWU, and told his supporters: 'Go to the archbishops and priests. Ask them for food and clothing.' When they responded with help, he resumed the free meals. When he wanted to, and when it suited his agenda, Connolly could be a pragmatic tactician.

The strike dragged on. Labour leaders, particularly in Britain, knew that Larkin and Connolly wanted an all-out sympathetic strike, but the leaders were much more circumspect, fearing they would be unleashing forces that would result in a general strike across Britain, with all the massive ramifications that would entail for the labour movement. Dublin, after all, was not their first priority, and they were deeply suspicious of the revolutionary instincts of Connolly and Larkin. More time passed and they began to withdraw support, funds dried up, the workers and their families began to starve, and the desperate started to drift back to work. In February 1914 the British Trades Union Congress announced there would be no more funds to help the Irish strikers.

'And so we Irish workers must go again down into Hell, bow our backs to the last of the slave drivers, let our hearts be seared by the iron of his hatred and instead of the sacramental wafer of brotherhood and common sacri-fice, eat the dust of defeat and betrayal. Dublin is isolated,' a furious Connolly wrote.[3] He would never trust the British labour movement again.

On the evening of 2 September 1913 two four-storey tenement houses in Dublin collapsed, killing seven and injuring others. The schoolteacher, barrister, writer, poet and Nationalist mystic Patrick Pearse, who normally had little interest in social conditions, wrote: 'The tenement houses of Dublin are so rotten that they periodically collapse on their inhabitants, and if the inhabitants collect in the street to discuss matters the police baton them to death ... Can you wonder that the protest is cruel and bloody.' Connolly welcomed these sentiments, and never forgot those of his fellow 1916 leaders who gave their support to the union during this period.

During the strike Captain Jack White, a former officer in the British Army and the son of a general, proposed the establishment of a trained and disciplined workers' defence force to protect strikers from aggressive 'scabs' and police. On 13 November a statement announcing the formation of an Irish Citizen Army was made. That evening, at a large meeting to celebrate Larkin's release from prison, Connolly declared: 'Listen to me, I am going to talk sedition. The next time we are out for a march, I want to be accompanied by four battalions of trained men with their corporals and sergeants and people to form fours. Why should we not train our men in Dublin as they are doing in Ulster?'[4] The strike led to enormous bitterness between the workers and the Dublin Metropolitan Police, whose strict no-nonsense approach to public disorder led to claims of brutality.

By drawing together diverse militant groups which had sprung up to resist Home Rule, the Ulster Volunteer Force was formed in January 1913, with the support of the Ulster Unionist Council. One hundred thousand-strong, well-financed and led by Lieutenant-General Sir George Richardson, a veteran of the Boxer Rebellion in China, it made clear that Unionist resistance to Home Rule was fiercely determined and not bound by constitutional methods.

By now there was real anger among supporters of Home Rule and a growing demand for a Nationalist counter-weight to the UVF. In response, the Irish Volunteers was formed in November 1913, following an article by Eoin MacNeill in the newspaper of the Gaelic League. MacNeill was a moderate Home Ruler who envisioned a volunteer force that would defend Home Rule if it was resisted by the UVF. His position was a defensive one, in the event of Britain failing to honour its obligation to Home Rule.

Ireland was militarising in response to the bitter divisions. Another, much older oath-bound revolutionary organisation, ever watchful for opportunity, covertly encouraged MacNeill to go ahead, and a provisional committee was quickly formed. MacNeill was a professor at the National University, vice president of the Gaelic League and an eminent scholar. He was the ideal frontman for the revolutionaries, who saw the new force as fertile ground for the recruitment of young Irishmen who were, in the main, not yet committed to armed insurrection.

MacNeill would later claim that he was aware of the role of the Irish Republican Brotherhood in the formation of the Irish Volunteers, but his relationship with the men who'd come from the IRB was never an easy one. They saw him as the respectable representative, but he was suspicious of their intentions and secrecy. He was too much the diffident academic to take effective action until it was too late. The scene was set for a confrontation over Home Rule, with the IRB positioning itself to take advantage of any opportunity.

In March 1914 a group of army officers at the Curragh military camp outside Dublin announced they would resign rather than fight Ulster's Unionists. Fearful that they could not rely on the army, the British Liberal government compromised, temporarily excluding part of the province of Ulster from the Home Rule Bill. Connolly saw this both as a betrayal and a stitch-up by the Liberals, the Irish Parliamentary Party and the Unionists. He simply did not believe that Ulster's Unionists could, or would, fight if Britain enforced Home Rule on all of Ireland.

On 24 April 1914 the UVF succeeded in purchasing and transporting from Germany about 30,000 rifles and five million rounds of ammunition to the Ulster port of Larne. They were now well equipped for any battle with Nationalist Ireland. On 26 July the Irish Volunteers landed around 1,500 rifles and 50,000 rounds of ammunition, also purchased in Germany, at Howth in County Dublin.

As the Volunteers were distributing the weapons in central Dublin a fracas developed with the army, which opened fire, killing three civilians.

The Irish Volunteers attracted many thousands of recruits, drawing from a broad spectrum across Nationalist Ireland. Over the years many Fenians and their supporters had fled or migrated to America, and along with large numbers of embittered post-famine Irish-Catholic emigrants had formed a 'nation across the sea'. The British home secretary between 1880 and 1885, Sir William Harcourt, had stated: 'There is an Irish nation in the United States, equally hostile, with plenty of money, absolutely beyond our reach and yet within ten days sail of our shore.'[5]

Once almost moribund, the Irish Republican Brotherhood was also beginning to reorganise, and in classic conspiratorial fashion began to infiltrate cultural organisations like the Gaelic League, dedicated to the restoration of the Gaelic language, and the Gaelic Athletic Association, which promoted Gaelic games. Much of this activity was the work of one man, Thomas Clarke, who had been sworn into the IRB in 1879 or 1880, when he was about twenty-one, and had come to the attention of the Royal Irish Constabulary shortly afterwards when he and some of his young comrades were involved in a fight with the police in Dungannon, County Tyrone. It was decided that Clarke should go to America, a well-worn route for IRB men forced out of Ireland.

Clarke arrived in New York in the early 1890s, and the

IRB provided him with an introduction to Clan na Gael.* The militant Irish-American scene at this time was a miasma of splits and conspiracy and was heavily penetrated by British intelligence, but in 1893 Clarke set sail for England to take part in a bombing campaign organised by Jeremiah O'Donovan Rossa, an exiled Fenian who had split from the main organisation. Clarke was quickly arrested, and on 14 June of that year he was sentenced to penal servitude for life.

After a successful campaign backed by many including notably John Redmond, Clarke was released. He married and returned to America where he resumed his association with Clan na Gael. Believing there would be war between the British and German Empires, and that this would provide the opportunity for another rebellion, he went back to Ireland in 1907. It is also likely that he was asked to return by John Devoy, the formidable leader of Clan na Gael. Fearful that Home Rule would satisfy most Irish people's desire for self-government and destroy their own dream of an independent Republic, both men were determined to smash the Bill at any cost.

Clarke was fiercely dedicated and disciplined and was the essential link between Devoy and Ireland. He bought a tobacconist shop in central Dublin, and from this small shop he set about the task of reorganising the IRB, talent-spotting and promoting men like Sean McDermott,

* Founded in 1867, the Clan recognised the IRB as the government of the Irish Republic.

his able deputy, whom he judged was ready to fight and die for an independent Irish Republic. All were sworn by oath to allegiance only to the IRB and to use any and every means to achieve their goal.

Another party was also beginning to make its presence felt. Sinn Fein is commonly regarded as having been founded in Dublin on 28 November 1905, and was the brainchild of Arthur Griffith, who initially favoured a policy of dual monarchy for Ireland, based on the Austria–Hungary model. During this period it was not a revolutionary party, and its position was one of passive resistance and abstentionism from Westminster. In fact, it was a very loose coalition held together by the industry of Griffith, and it had a brand: the words 'Sinn Fein', meaning 'Ourselves alone', a slogan taken from the Gaelic League. Sinn Fein came to be used as a sort of shorthand or umbrella term for those who wanted separation from Great Britain. It should also be said that while for many people the Easter Rising quickly became known as the Sinn Fein Rising, and although individual members of the party took part in it, Sinn Fein as an organisation was not involved. It was only after the Rising that Sinn Fein rose to prominence and became a totally different movement.

And where was Connolly in all this? Although broadly supportive, he had little time for the largely bourgeois leadership of the Irish Volunteers, or indeed for what was going on in other political parties. His life during this period was still dominated by the strike and by the struggle to keep the ITGWU together and focused in the aftermath of their defeat.

Events in Europe were beginning to overshadow the so-called Irish Problem. On 4 August 1914 Britain declared war on Germany, and the Home Rule Bill, which had finally succeeded in being ratified by Parliament, was shelved in its entirety for one year or until the war was won, whichever came soonest. This was the high point of Irish constitutional Nationalism: Redmond had succeeded where Parnell had failed. But the Bill was now delayed and also included the promise of an amending Bill to deal with Ulster. This would mean Unionists could opt out. In the interim, Redmond's supporters had taken many of the senior positions in the Irish Volunteers, much to the IRB's disgust, and were ready to support the British war effort in return for Home Rule when the war ended.

Connolly was now hell-bent on an armed revolt, and a meeting was arranged for September 1914. He would not have known which of them were members of the IRB owing to their oath of secrecy, but the meeting was chaired by Tom Clarke, and present were Pearse, McDermott, Joseph Plunkett and Eamonn Ceannt. It was agreed that they should plan for a rebellion before the war ended, and it was decided to open communications with Germany through their Irish-American contacts.

When, on 20 September, Redmond called on the Irish Volunteers to fight for Britain – or perhaps more precisely, the British Empire – the organisation split. One hundred thousand men sided with Redmond and now called themselves the National Volunteers, though around 11,000 rejected Redmond's call. Keeping the name Irish Volunteers, they re-formed under the nominal command of Eoin MacNeill.* In October the Irish Volunteers were again reorganised and key positions went to IRB members including Pearse, Thomas MacDonagh and Plunkett. Clarke, as ever, remained in the background. Connolly meanwhile retained complete control of the Irish Citizen Army. Revolution was becoming more than a dream.

In the meantime, unsurprisingly perhaps, Larkin and Connolly were at loggerheads. Both were thin-skinned egoists and eager to see slights where none were intended. Eventually Larkin left for America in September 1914, and was once again imprisoned because of his socialist and pro-German activities. He was not to return to Ireland until 1923. Connolly took over as general secretary of the ITGWU, editor of the *Irish Worker* and commander of the ICA against Larkin's strongest wishes.

The conspirators in the IRB were emboldened. Perhaps once again England's difficulty would be Ireland's opportunity. Militant Irish Nationalism had long sought foreign help for its cause, and now it was the turn of imperial Germany to be lobbied for assistance. The list would go on to include Soviet Russia, Nazi Germany and, in the

* MacNeill was not a member of the IRB, and knew little of their intentions or of their growing influence within his organisation.

years to come, Libya, East Germany, the PLO, Hamas and Saddam's Ba'ath Party.

Many of the Irish Volunteers still thought Connolly too extreme, and, to his fury, a formal pact between the Volunteers and the IRB proved impossible. Connolly thought moderate Home Rulers still controlled the Volunteers, but it was not as simple as that. The majority of the Volunteers were in favour of a revolt only as a response to any attempt to introduce conscription in Ireland. Most of the IRB men wanted a revolt when the time was right and only if all other options failed. But a third group, clustered around Pearse and Clarke, was impatient to strike. Connolly was unsure who to trust but, of them all, he was warming to Pearse. Unlike most of his IRB comrades, Pearse preached the gospel of revolution openly, and, like Connolly, he was a fine writer and an even more charismatic orator.

Connolly was often excluded from the councils of the IRB, which added to his frustration. However, they did at times co-operate; for instance, when Nora Connolly was sent to America in late 1914 with a very secret message for the leaders there. But such close co-operation was rare, and perhaps owed more to Nora's age, which meant she was unlikely to be suspected, and that she had lived there and knew her way around.

In August 1915 the body of O'Donovan Rossa was returned to Ireland from America. All past differences were forgotten and the IRB began to organise the funeral. John Devoy and Tom Clarke took control and set about orchestrating a show of strength. They chose Patrick Pearse to give the oration. Determined that the IRB should make a public statement, Clarke instructed Pearse to throw caution to the winds, and Pearse rose to the occasion. The result was at once mystical, lyrical and passionate, and is still regarded by many militant Republicans as one of the most revered statements of Irish Nationalism. It is perhaps best remembered for one passage: 'The fools, the fools, they have left us our Fenian dead, and while Ireland holds these graves, Ireland unfree shall never be at peace.'*

It was a great piece of propaganda. A huge crowd attended the funeral, and many Nationalist organisations were represented, including the Irish Citizen Army. For many spectators it was the sight of armed men and the volley of shots over O'Rossa's grave that commanded their attention. 'The funeral was most impressive, skilfully organised and carried out,' Father Curran, secretary to the Catholic Archbishop of Dublin, noted in his diary. 'It was a challenge to Dublin Castle and a deeply significant lesson to the Irish people.'[6]

The volley of shots was more than a farewell to an old Fenian. It was a sign of defiance to England by a new generation in Ireland, and both it and, more especially, the oration have reverberated through Nationalist Ireland

* Pearse was using 'Fenian' here as a metaphor for all those who had 'died for Ireland'. The truth is that very few actual Fenians or Irish revolutionaries had died in battle after the revolt of 1798.

for a hundred years. For me and other members of my generation it was holy writ, and I could recite it by heart before I was in my teens.

After Larkin's departure, Connolly exerted a vice-like grip over the ICA and the union, becoming somewhat of a dictator. In the months before the Rising, he turned Liberty Hall into an apparent armed camp and munitions factory. Members of the union executive were dismayed at Connolly's behaviour in general and particularly the takeover of Liberty Hall by his ICA. Just days before the Rising they finally faced him down. He agreed to leave Liberty Hall within days and not return. Unlike the executive, Connolly knew the Rising was just days away and accepted their decision. It is without doubt that if Larkin had not gone to America, Connolly could never have controlled Liberty Hall as he did. Events may well have turned out very differently.

From now until January 1916 Connolly would goad the Volunteer leadership privately and publicly, alleging they were just talkers and not serious about revolt. He would sometimes threaten to go it alone with the ICA. Concerned that he might well do something rash or provoke a response from the authorities, the IRB decided to act.

Chapter 5

THE RISING

At lunchtime on Wednesday 19 January 1916, Connolly received a message at Liberty Hall that Pearse, McDermott and Plunkett, all members of the military council of the IRB, wished to speak with him and that a car was waiting.

Friends and colleagues heard nothing more from Connolly and were unaware of where he was until he arrived at Surrey House, the residence of Constance Markievicz, on Saturday night, 22 January. There is still doubt about what exactly took place during those three missing days. Fearing that Connolly had been kidnapped by the Volunteers, Markievicz wanted to mobilise the ICA and rescue him by force. Wiser counsel prevailed.

The previous Christmas Pearse had described the relationship between the Volunteers and Connolly as a state of 'armed neutrality'. Speaking to Desmond Ryan, a close colleague, he said, 'Connolly is most dishonest in his methods. He will never be satisfied until he goads us into action, and then he will think most of us too moderate, and want to guillotine half of us. I can see him setting up a guillotine, can't you? For [John Bulmer] Hobson and [Eoin] MacNeill in particular. They are poles apart.'[1] In a clear reference to Connolly, MacNeill wrote in the *Irish Volunteer* on 25 December 1915: 'No man has a right to seek relief of his own feelings at the expense of his country.'

During the three days that Connolly was closeted with the IRB leaders they finally took him into their confidence. Angry at first at his treatment, he became so ecstatic that he could hardly be persuaded to leave. They discussed the details for the Rising, pooling their ideas and plans until eventually arriving at a common purpose.

When Connolly returned to Surrey House Markievicz asked him where he had been. He replied rather melodramatically: 'I have been in hell, but I conquered my conquerors.' Geraldine Plunkett, sister of Joseph, wrote later that when Plunkett returned home exhausted, he exclaimed, 'My God, what an extraordinary man James Connolly is.'[2]

In spite of their respect for him, Connolly's antagonising of IRB leaders and the more level-headed of the Volunteer military leaders is well documented. Certainly MacNeill thought him a short-sighted and reckless amateur. And as Darrell Figgis also points out in his *Recollections of the Irish War*, 'It was he who was mainly responsible during Easter Week for the mistaken strategy of occupying public buildings that were the target for artillery. He believed that the capitalist class of one country would never destroy the buildings that were the pride of the capitalist class of another.'[3]

Connolly was clear about what he wanted and he had forced the IRB into a union. There would be a revolt, a rising, and he and his ICA would be equal partners with the IRB. The forces of extreme Nationalism and socialism would be as one in the struggle for national liberation. This does not mean that he had relegated socialism to a secondary position; in fact, nothing could be further from reality.

Connolly and the secret military council of the IRB, of which he was now a member, decided a rising would take place on Easter Sunday 1916, and that Pearse, as director of organisation, should coordinate manoeuvres by the Volunteers throughout the country on the day. This would provide a cover for the real plan, which was to stage a countrywide armed revolt.

Accordingly the *Irish Volunteer* carried an order from Pearse that 'following the lines of last year, every unit of the Irish Volunteers will hold manoeuvres during the Easter Holidays. The object of the exercise is to test manoeuvres with equipment.' This order was issued with the approval of the Volunteer executive and the chief of staff, Eoin MacNeill. They were, however, unaware of the secret orders Pearse had issued to brigade commandants who were under the control of the IRB.

Connolly urged the IRB to seize the principal public buildings in Dublin and occupy the city, arguing that a swift strike at the heart of the enemy would be the most effective strategy; his plan prevailed despite misgivings on the part of the other members of the IRB executive. It did so primarily because on the day both the ICA and the Volunteers were lacking in numbers, organisation, experience and weaponry and were confined to Dublin.

The ICA was about 800 strong and fewer than 200 took part in the Rising. By contrast, around 2–3,000 members of the ITGWU had volunteered to fight for the British Empire in the Great War, although the actual figure is still disputed. Along with everything else, this was a very bitter pill for Connolly to swallow, especially as many of the first men to have signed up were themselves veterans of the 1913 strike.

In his autobiography *Silent Years,* John Francis Byrne wrote that Connolly's plan was 'worse than foolish. The total number of insurrectionists in Dublin was at no time greater than seven hundred, yet they took up their stand in a city in which the great majority of the citizens were unsympathetic, if not hostile. The city of Dublin was a position wholly indefensible. Half a dozen British warships would have demolished the city in a day. A few pieces of artillery of small calibre actually did demolish the chief rebel strongholds in a couple of hours.'[4]

It is now known from many sources, including British intelligence agencies, that the authorities in Dublin Castle knew a lot about the preparations for the Rising. The Naval Intelligence Division in London was intercepting messages between Berlin and the German embassy in Washington, which included contributions from John Devoy, the leader of Clan na Gael in America. They were, however, unsure how to deal with it. Intelligence information was also pointing clearly towards a landing of German munitions on the south-west coast and an armed revolt on the Easter weekend of 1916. Yet still the authorities based in Dublin Castle dithered, worried that any action against the IRB leaders would make the situation worse. In November 1915 the chief secretary for Ireland wrote that to take notice of 'crackpot priests and other enthusiasts would only halt the growth of loyalty in Ireland'.

A letter dated 17 April 1916, from the general in charge of the defence of the South of Ireland to the under-secretary of state, confirmed that a landing of arms was expected on the south-west coast and a rising fixed for Easter weekend. The information received could hardly have been more specific, but nothing was done.

Germany had indeed sent assistance, but it fell far short of what the IRB hoped for. There were a number of reasons for this, among them the particularly inept performance of Sir Roger Casement, who went to Berlin in 1914 to lobby for German recognition of an independent Irish Republic and military assistance to establish it. He succeeded in his first aim when he secured a treaty giving formal recognition to Ireland's right to independence, and which was endorsed by the German chancellor, von Bethmann Hollweg.

Casement was one of the most exotic and erratic characters ever to grace the Irish revolutionary stage. Born near Dublin in 1864 and brought up in a Protestant family in Ulster, he became one of Henry Morton Stanley's volunteers in the newly created Congo Free State. He went on to serve as British consul there, and then in 1904 produced a sensational report which showed how the Congo Free State was being run with unrelenting cruelty for the personal profit of King Leopold II of Belgium. Six years later, after a visit to the Upper Amazon, he provided an even more horrific account of how natives were being maltreated by the Peruvian Amazon Company, a British-registered firm. For these services Casement was granted a knighthood. He then became an Irish Republican, for reasons that are somewhat impenetrable and beyond the scope of this book.

Once the First World War broke out Casement's sympathies were entirely with Germany. First he went to America, where he met with John Devoy, who was already in contact with Germany. When Casement suggested that he go there as an envoy, Devoy reluctantly agreed. Eventually, after a comic attempt by Casement to recruit Irish POWs in German camps and form an Irish brigade to fight in the Rising, the German High Command began to ignore him and communicated directly with Devoy.

Germany had every reason to want a successful revolt in Ireland but it had many demands on its resources, not least in the killing fields of northern France. But Casement was convinced that without a German commitment in the form of officers and weapons any revolt in Ireland was madness. This view was shared by most of the leadership of the Volunteers, including MacNeill and several senior members of the IRB, but not by its military council, or by Connolly.

On 19 April 1916 a Norwegian-registered trawler called the *Aud* set sail for Ireland with 20,000 rifles, ammunition and ten machine guns. There were no German soldiers on board because none could be spared. Casement had persuaded the Germans to send him to Ireland, and also to provide him with a submarine. They were, in truth, glad to be rid of him. Casement also hoped to get word to MacNeill to cancel the Rising, believing that without German officers and far more weaponry they were doomed to failure.

Having been intercepting communications between Berlin and the German embassy in Washington for some time, the Admiralty was well aware of the IRB's plan. Yet even it could not have predicted the series of disasters that would now unfold.

First, the *Aud* had no wireless and so failed to receive a message that the rendezvous off the west coast of Ireland had been delayed. Second, when it reached Tralee Bay there was no one there to meet it. Eventually the *Aud* aroused suspicion and was escorted to Cork harbour by the British Navy. The captain then lowered the lifeboats and scuttled his ship. Casement was put ashore from the submarine near Tralee, but he too was captured and eventually taken to London, where he was tried for treason, found guilty and hanged.

On hearing of the capture of the *Aud*, as well as learning that he had been lied to repeatedly by Pearse and his associates, MacNeill wrote a statement for the national newspaper, the *Sunday Independent*, which counter-manded Pearse's previous instructions to the Volunteers. This, combined with similar messages, caused confusion in the Volunteers' ranks and finished any possibility, however ill-planned and militarily naive, of a countrywide revolt.

The clear evidence of the Volunteers' collusion with Germany now led the British viceroy, Lord Wimborne, to insist that sixty or more of the leaders be arrested. Wimborne, however, postponed making the arrests until after permission had been received from the chief secretary in London, which did not arrive until Easter Monday. If the leaders had been arrested on Saturday evening, or even on Sunday morning, there would surely have been no Rising. It is one of the great what ifs of Irish history.

Knowing of MacNeill's countermanding order and the capture of the *Aud*, the seven members of the IRB military council met on Sunday morning at Liberty Hall. The IRB's plans for a major revolt were in ruins. They knew now that they would certainly be arrested, Rising or not. They had to make a decision. To sit and await arrest was to invite ridicule and lose face for ever. To go ahead meant certain defeat and likely death, but it also held out the possibility of glory. Deciding that the Rising should be postponed until noon Easter Monday, they sent word to this effect to as many men as possible. Connolly and Thomas MacDonagh then organised the printing of the 'Proclamation of the Irish Republic' on the presses of the *Irish Worker*. Connolly undoubtedly made a large contribution to the final draft, which declared 'the right of the people of Ireland to the ownership of Ireland'. It also declared its commitment to 'the happiness and prosperity of the whole nation and all of its parts', a phrase that had been used by Connolly on previous occasions.

But who or what did these seven men stand for? The short answer is no one but themselves. They were totally self-appointed, and did not even represent a majority within the Volunteers or the IRB membership. The Proclamation describes them as 'The Provisional Government of the Irish Republic', and then goes on to claim authority 'in the name of God and of the dead generations'. It further states that 'The Irish Republic is entitled to, and hereby claims, the allegiance of every Irishman and Irishwoman.'

God and the dead generations, both of whom we can assume were not asked for their opinion, were all the authority these men could or would invoke as justification for their actions. They also demanded allegiance because they were now the 'Government of the Republic'. This is the language of a military putsch.

In my opinion, this Proclamation is the sacred text that

authorises any group of terrorist fascists to murder in the pursuit or defence of a mythical Republic. The IRA, the Provisional IRA, the INLA, the Real IRA, the Continuity IRA – they all acted, and are acting, in the same spirit as the men of 1916. An all-Ireland Republic has still not been achieved, and this Proclamation is what ultimately gives authority to so-called dissident groups today. At the time of writing, the fastest growing dissident grouping in Northern Ireland is called the 1916 Societies.

At 11.45 a.m. on Easter Monday a bugle sounded outside Liberty Hall and the men and women of the Irish Citizen Army fell in. The main body of the ICA, some hundred-strong, commanded by Michael Mallon and including a number of women and young Fianna boy scouts, marched off to St Stephen's Green. Shortly after midday a group of men from the ICA approached Dublin Castle, the heart of the British administration in Ireland. Constable James O'Brien of the Dublin Metropolitan Police stood alone and unarmed at the public entrance to the castle. As the armed men attempted to push through, O'Brien blocked them, and Sean Connolly (no relation) shot him in the head. The first victim of the Rising – an Irishman, a Catholic and almost certainly a Nationalist – died instantly. According to Fearghal McGarry, Connolly's Citizen Army were more ruthless than the Volunteers when it came to shooting members of the Dublin Metropolitan Police, which was an unarmed police service. Asked how they should deal with the DMP, one ICA officer recalled

Connolly's reply: 'Remember how they treated you in 1913 [during the lock-out]?'[5]

The rest, together with about seventy Irish Volunteers and Connolly's only son, fifteen-year-old Roddy, fell in behind three commandants-general appointed by the military council the previous Saturday. In the centre was James Connolly, to his right Patrick Pearse, and to his left Joseph Plunkett, who unsheathed his sabre as he took up position.

They were followed by men mostly without uniforms, many dressed in their work clothes. A number of vehicles loaded with an assortment of arms and explosives brought up the rear. Thomas Clarke and Sean McDermott walked along the footpath.

They set off down Lower Abbey Street and into O'Connell Street. As they reached the GPO the Angelus bell rang out from the nearby cathedral, Connolly shouted 'Charge', and amid much confusion they stormed into the General Post Office. In O'Connell Street two unarmed policemen of the Dublin Metropolitan Police strolled by in the sunshine. Meanwhile, in St Stephen's Green the ICA began to build barricades. One elderly man was shot dead after trying repeatedly to remove his commandeered lorry from a barricade near the Shelbourne Hotel. The Irish Citizen Army was responsible for several dubious deaths of civilians in this area.

Minutes before the GPO was stormed, Arthur Hamilton Norway, the head of the General Post Office in Ireland, was in his office, where he had an automatic pistol belonging to his nineteen-year-old son, recently killed on the Western Front.* It proved to be the only loaded gun in the GPO; the guards had all been issued with guns but no ammunition. Called to a meeting in Dublin Castle to discuss the arrest of the leaders of the Irish Volunteers with senior government and army officials, he was within hearing distance when Constable O'Brien was shot dead.

Having secured the GPO, Pearse and Connolly went to the foot of Nelson's Pillar in O'Connell Street, where Pearse read out the Proclamation to about four hundred generally bemused Dubliners. Most people in the vicinity did not have a clue what was going on: there had been no obvious increase in tension, no sense that something dramatic was in the air. Some reports have Pearse reading out sections of the Proclamation a second time, since some listeners did not understand it. The author and poet James Stephens, who was in Dublin that week and witnessed this event, wrote: 'None of these people had been prepared for insurrection. The thing had been sprung on them so quickly they were unable to take sides.'[6]

One of the first casualties of the Rising on the British side was Lieutenant Gerald Neilan of the Royal Dublin Fusiliers, whose younger brother, Anthony, was fighting with the Irish Volunteers. Thousands of Irishmen were fighting and dying on the Western Front, Catholic and Protestant, Nationalist and Unionist; it has also been

---

* Another son was the novelist Nevil Shute.

pointed out that the total number of men from both the Irish Volunteers and the ICA involved in the Rising comprised less than 1 per cent of the total number of Irishmen who served in the British Army during the First World War.

The inhabitants of Dublin's plentiful slums now took advantage of the occasion to engage in systematic looting.* Attempts by the Volunteers to stop them failed. Even shots fired over their heads did not deter them. The looters presented the Volunteers with a serious problem since many were fiercely hostile and, when drunk, seemed determined to attack them. Both Pearse and Connolly talked half-heartedly about shooting some of the looters, but this was more an attempt to boost the morale of their men, who were shaken by the levels of aggression directed their way.

At around 3 p.m. the next day (Tuesday) the distant boom of artillery could be heard. This was the last thing Connolly expected, and according to witnesses he was visibly taken aback. Early on the Wednesday morning word reached the GPO that a gunboat had come up the River Liffey and was lobbing shells at Liberty Hall, which was now empty apart from a caretaker. Hearing the report, one Volunteer said to another, 'General Connolly told us the British would never use artillery against us.' To which the second Volunteer replied, 'He did, did he? Wouldn't it be

---

* After the Rising ended more than 400 Dubliners were charged with looting, stealing and general vandalism.

great now if General Connolly was making the decisions for the British?'[7]

Frank Henderson, an officer in the Irish Volunteers who was engaged in fighting in other parts of the city, recalls that he received a message from Connolly on the Tuesday evening ordering them to make their way to the GPO. He remembers that Sean Russell was among his party. Russell, later the IRA chief of staff, would die on a German U-boat in 1940 returning from Nazi Germany with plans for an IRA revolt in Ireland.

Eventually, after much difficulty, the Volunteers reached the front of the GPO, where confused firing broke out between them and Volunteers stationed in the nearby Imperial Hotel who were holding prisoners still dressed in British Army uniform. Men on both sides were injured before Connolly dashed out onto the road with his arms raised and shouting to his men in the Imperial Hotel to stop firing, which they did.

There is no doubt that Connolly showed personal bravery during the Rising, nor is there any doubt that he was in charge. On the Thursday he decided to set up new outposts, and led a group of men into Prince's Street, where they began to build a barricade with whatever they could find. Connolly supervised the work, striding back and forth and seemingly oblivious to heavy gunfire being directed at them.

Instructing his men to stay where they were, he walked briskly back from Prince's Street to the GPO. He went to the hospital section and removed his coat, revealing a flesh wound in his arm. The wound was dressed and Connolly left, warning sternly that nothing was to be said about this. Returning to the barricades, a bullet shattered his left ankle, whereupon he dragged himself into Prince's Street, where he fell flat in the gutter.

He was carried into the GPO and treated by Lieutenant Mahoney, a captured British Army doctor from Cork, who applied a tourniquet to the wound. Remaining conscious but in great pain throughout the rest of the day, Connolly was given several injections of morphine procured from a pharmacy in Henry Street.

The next day (Friday) Connolly insisted on being transferred to a bed with castors so that he could move among the men in the main hall of the GPO. In a last written message Pearse paid a special tribute to Connolly, who 'lies wounded but is still the guiding brain of our resistance'. By 4 p.m. fires had spread along O'Connell Street and all the buildings were burning. Incendiary shells rained on the GPO, and Connolly told his men that the British were at last about to make their frontal assault. But when McDermott ordered the removal of all the wounded to Jervis Street Hospital Connolly refused to go, saying he had to stay with his men. Pearse and Connolly also decreed that all the women in the GPO should be evacuated, although two nurses and Connolly's secretary, Winifred Carney, insisted on staying with him and the other wounded.

At about six o'clock that evening the leaders gathered around Connolly's bed to work out an evacuation plan of the GPO, which was now in flames. Yet it was not until the Saturday morning that they escaped via holes dug through the walls until they reached 16 Moore Street. All of this was agonising for Connolly as his shattered ankle had turned gangrenous and any movement was unbearable. In a hopeless position in Moore Street, they decided to seek terms from the British Army.

At 11.45 on Saturday morning a nurse named Elizabeth O'Farrell walked towards the British Army barricade at the top of Moore Street and spoke with a British Army officer, saying the men wanted to treat. 'Go and tell Mr Pearse that I will not treat at all unless he surrenders unconditionally,' the officer responded. 'Tell him also that when he comes here Mr Connolly must follow on a stretcher.'[8] Winifred Carney asked Connolly if there was any other way to end the Rising. He replied, 'I cannot bear to see all these brave boys burn to death. There is no other way.' He was then taken under armed guard to an infirmary in Dublin Castle.

Connolly had always been clear that he believed both he and the other signatories to the Proclamation would be executed.

On Monday 1 May he made his confession to a Catholic priest and the following day received Holy Communion. There has long been dispute about the strengths of Connolly's religious beliefs, but there is no doubt that he took confession and communion before his execution. In a letter to his close colleague John Matheson in December

1907, in reply to a direct question, he wrote: 'For myself tho' I have usually posed as a Catholic I have not gone to my duty for 15 years and have not the slightest tincture of faith left.'[9] He knew, though, that to be a self-proclaimed atheist in that period in Ireland was to forgo any influence in public life. It also seems to have meant something to him culturally in terms of being Irish. But beyond this he appears quite prepared to dissemble, if only so as not to give his enemies any further ammunition to use against him. It is clear from his writings that he did not believe either the practice or observance of religion were barriers to being a Marxist. But his private reply in 1907 to Matheson, whom he trusted, should be remembered, and the fact that he was just as prepared to lie for the cause as he was to die for it.

On Tuesday 2 May Lillie Connolly, accompanied by their nine-year-old daughter Fiona, born in America, visited Connolly in Dublin Castle Hospital. It is unclear when they had last seen each other before this visit. On Tuesday 9 May, Lillie, along with Nora, again visited her husband. That morning Connolly had been court-martialled and sentenced to death by firing squad. He advised his family to go to America, and asked Nora to arrange publication of his songs and give the proceeds to her mother. He seemed to regard Nora as the adult in the relationship, or perhaps Lillie was too distraught for conversation of this nature.

At midnight on Thursday 11 May Lillie was called on by an army officer, who told her that her husband wished to see his wife and eldest daughter once more. Nora described the last conversation between her mother and father.

'Well, Lillie, I suppose you know what this means?'

'James, James. It's not that – it's not,' Mama wailed.

'Yes, Lillie,' he said, patting her hand. 'I fell asleep tonight for the first time. I was awakened at eleven and told I was to be shot at dawn.'

Mama was kneeling, her head on the bed, sobbing heart-breakingly.

Daddy laid his hand on her head. 'Don't cry, Lillie,' he pleaded. 'You'll unman me.'

'But your beautiful life, James,' Mama sobbed. 'Your beautiful life.'

'Hasn't it been a full life, Lillie,' he said. 'And isn't this a good end?'[10]

It was certainly not the end for Lillie Connolly, who was left a penniless widow with six living children. Permission for her family to return to America was refused, and she subsequently converted to Catholicism, some sources say on Connolly's urging, later joining the Legion of Mary, a Roman Catholic lay organisation.

About a month after Connolly's execution his elder brother John died in Edinburgh. A former British Army soldier, he was buried with full military honours.

Chapter 6

AFTERMATH: 1916–23

While Connolly was still in hospital in Dublin Castle, during Lillie and Nora's visit on 9 May he was anxious for news of how the Rising was being viewed.

'Have you seen any socialist papers?' he asked Nora. 'They [the socialists] will never understand why I am here,' he remarked. 'They will all forget I am an Irishman.'[1]

Connolly was right: they did not understand. The Independent Labour Party did not support him, although the Glasgow branch of the British Socialist Party did, and united behind him. *Forward* was against, declaring Connolly's participation 'a mystery', and the Socialist Labour Party he had co-founded was hopelessly split. Every single British Labour person of even trifling significance was opposed to what he had done, as was every periodical and newspaper. The *Irish Times* and the

William Martin Murphy-owned *Irish Independent* were also profoundly against and militant in their calls for the rebels to be treated harshly, as were the leaders of constitutional Irish Nationalism. Writing in *Justice*, John Leslie, Connolly's first mentor – and the man whose public plea to socialists had provided him with his first job in Ireland – was horrified, dismissing the Rising as 'sad, mad and bad'.[2]

Immediately following the surrender many of the Volunteers were in a state of extremely low morale. This description of a relatively senior IRB man (Con Colbert, later executed for his part in the Rising) by one of his command during their immediate detention in Richmond Barracks is striking: 'He [Colbert] said that from his point of view he would prefer to be executed and said "We are all ready to meet our God." We had hopes of coming out alive. Now that we are defeated, outside that barrack wall, the people whom we have tried to emancipate have demonstrated nothing but hate and contempt for us.'[3]

In my opinion 'hate and contempt' was not the universal view of people in Dublin and certainly not in the rest of Ireland. Anger and bewilderment is perhaps a better description: Nationalist feeling ran too strong in parts of Ireland and in much of the Irish psyche for it to be as straightforward as that. To believe that the Irish at first hated the rebels, and then became supporters within weeks of the executions, is too simplistic.

As Charles Townshend makes clear in his brilliantly lucid book *Easter 1916: The Irish Rebellion*, the reaction was rather more mixed, although more is known about those of the middle-class because most of them were letter-writers or diarists.

The author James Stephens, who was present in Dublin during the Rising, and made it his business to get around and listen, has some of the most interesting observations of the mood. 'Men met and talked volubly of course but they said nothing that indicated a personal desire or belief.' The main view was simply one of 'astonishment at the suddenness and completeness of the occurrence ... The idea at first among the people had been that the insurrection would be ended the morning after it began. But today, the insurrection having lasted three days, people are ready to concede that it may last forever.' Moreover, there was almost a feeling of gratitude towards the Volunteers for 'holding out for a little while, for had they been beaten on the first or second day, the city would have been humiliated to the soul'.[4]

It is understandable that there should have been mixed feelings since the majority of Irish people, with the exception of Unionists, wanted self-governance. This does not mean that they supported the Rising – most of them emphatically did not – but they knew where the rebels were coming from, and, as always in Ireland in such circumstances, there were emotional nerve endings just under the surface waiting to be ignited.

Anyone who lived through the period of the 1981 IRA hunger strike at the Maze prison, during which ten men died, will have a sense of what I mean. About eight weeks before Bobby Sands died there was a demonstration in support of the prisoners in my home town of Tralee in which only thirteen people participated. On the day of Sands's funeral, however, most shops and businesses in the town closed and about 5,000 people marched in support of the hunger strikers, including a member of parliament, local councillors, priests, nuns, business people and so on. The march was led by a uniformed IRA colour party as the police looked on. To show its non-sectarian nature, the proceedings began with a decade of the Rosary. Even though I was by then an agent of the Garda Siochana, it fell to me to address the crowd. I remember seeing one TD kneeling on the ground in front of the IRA colour party as the Rosary was being recited.

I recall feeling deeply uncomfortable with what was happening around me, and hating what I considered to be the sanctimonious ethnic-fuelled drivel being peddled. Yet I also knew that, for most of those in attendance, the emotional solidarity with the strikers would fade quickly. Most of them did not support the Provisional IRA campaign, but that would not bother the IRA, who would trumpet sympathy for the strikers as support for the Long War. The IRA has always sought to describe the hunger strikes of the early 1980s as 'our 1916', and it is not hard to see why. This was and remains murky and disturbing ground.

The future leader of the labour movement in Ireland, and no supporter of the Rising, Thomas Johnson, found a similar reaction among the people of Drogheda on the Thursday of that week in 1916, where there was little sign of sympathy with the rebels, but instead a general admiration for their courage and strategy.

A total of 3,430 men and seventy-nine women were arrested after the Rising, and of these 1,424 men and seventy-three women were subsequently released. Of almost 2,000 men who were sent to be interned in England, over 1,200 were quickly returned home when the authorities decided they were unimportant, or indeed innocent. Most of the others were home by Christmas 1916 and all freed under a general amnesty in July 1917.

However, it was decided that 170 men and one woman, Constance Markievicz, were to be court-martialled. Almost everything about the courts martial has long been controversial in Ireland, and the controversies continue to this day. Were they properly constituted? Were the military officers deputed as judges competent? Was there adequate provision for the defendants' defence? And so on.

Once they had surrendered unconditionally, all the signatories to the Proclamation expected to be executed. These were harsh times. The First World War was still raging, and the British Empire was engaged in a terrible struggle for its survival. Whatever the rights or wrongs, and Home Rule had after all been achieved, it was simply too much to ask that an attempted revolt against Britain, with assistance from its enemy, would be met with tolerance or leniency. Prime Minister Asquith publicly said that the government's paramount duty was to stamp out rebellion with 'all possible vigour and promptitude', and it did.

All the defendants, with the exception of Sir Roger Casement, faced one central charge. That they 'did an act, to wit did take part in an armed rebellion and in the waging of war against His Majesty the King, such act being of such a nature as to be calculated to be prejudicial to the defence of the realm, being done with the intention and for the purpose of Easter Rising, assisting the enemy'.[5]

Between 30 April and 17 May, 160 prisoners were tried by the field general court martial. The trials were held in camera, none of the prisoners were represented and none were allowed to give sworn evidence in their defence. Ninety death sentences were passed, and of these fifteen were carried out.

The first death sentence was passed on 2 May. Rather bizarrely, because they were being court-martialled and not tried by civil courts, which had been suspended, it was necessary to prove that a defendant had acted 'with the intention of assisting the enemy' before the death penalty could be invoked. This was turning out to be difficult until Patrick Pearse, a trained barrister, intervened.

On 1 May, Pearse wrote a letter to his mother, which was seized and produced at his trial. After finishing the letter, he added a postscript which he placed at the head of the first page where it could hardly be overlooked by his captors, in which he said that he believed that the German fleet had set sail but had been defeated by the British. This would form the cornerstone of the British case. In his address at his trial Pearse once again emphasised German involvement, thus implicating everyone involved in the Rising. The rebel leaders were therefore accused of being in alliance with Germany while thousands of Irishmen, Unionist and Nationalist, were fighting side by side against it. The result was that the centre of Dublin, the second city of the British Empire, had been reduced to ruins. Unionists, most constitutional Nationalists and the British and Irish papers called for stern action against them.

Home Rule, the subject of years of parliamentary battle, was finally on the statute book, though postponed for the duration of the war, and everyone of any substance, intelligence or influence on either side of the Irish Sea knew that the partition of Ireland was inevitable, Nationalists hoped temporarily. Only the precise size of the respective territories was yet to be decided.

So what to do with the leaders? Give them a clip round the ear and send them home? There is a case to be made that says this is what happened to the other men and women who were sentenced to various terms of penal servitude, some up to life, yet were all released within eighteen months.

On 3 May 1916 Pearse, Clarke and MacDonagh were executed. It can truly be said of Pearse that this was what he craved. Any other result would have deeply disappointed him. Perhaps only death by public hanging – like his hero Robert Emmet – with all its pageantry would have been more satisfactory for him.

As more executions followed, the public and political mood in Ireland became ever more fractious. There was now intense disagreement among those charged with administering Ireland, who were broadly urging caution, and General John Maxwell, who had been sent in to crush the rebellion and deal with the aftermath. While not the ogre or social reactionary often caricatured in Ireland, he was a soldier determined to follow his instructions from the British government. He was obviously perplexed by the moderate Irish Nationalists and the confusing signals he felt they sent out. Having called for strong action against the rebel leaders, some were now fiercely criticising the government for the executions.

As early as 3 May, after the first executions, the leader of the Irish Parliamentary Party, John Redmond, was making his views clear to Prime Minister Asquith: 'If any more executions take place in Ireland, the position will become impossible for any Constitutional Party or leader.'[6] And on 8 May, John Dillon, deputy leader of the Irish Parliamentary Party, also told General Maxwell that it really would be difficult to exaggerate the mischief the executions were doing.

Martial law was now in force across the entire country and searches for weapons and arrests were commonplace.

Ireland is a small country and restrictions on reporting let loose a torrent of lurid rumour. Fifty people had been executed, and summary executions were becoming a regular occurrence in Dublin.

On Wednesday 10 May, General Maxwell confirmed the verdict of the courts martial of Connolly and McDermott, and sent a message to the British cabinet that both men would be executed the following morning. Asquith responded that no more executions were to take place until further orders – but these, the last of the executions, were allowed to go ahead on 12 May.

On 11 May, John Dillon erupted in a dramatic intervention in the House of Commons. 'You are washing out our whole life work in a sea of blood,' he declared. 'What is poisoning the mind of Ireland, and rapidly poisoning it, is the secrecy of these trials and the continuance of these executions.' Thousands of people in Dublin who ten days previously had been opposed to the whole Sinn Fein movement and the rebellion were now in danger of becoming resentful of the government.[7]

It is in Dillon's next words and the reaction of other parliamentarians to them that an all-too-familiar ethnic (or as Maxwell said, racial) gulf becomes clear. Dillon was an Irishman. He wanted self-government or Home Rule for Ireland. Though loath to admit it, he knew that this would exclude some or all of Ulster, at least temporarily. And he knew the hard core of the rebels wanted a Republic, but he was also convinced that the majority of the rebels and the Irish people would settle for less, as they did when the Anglo-Irish Treaty was agreed after the War of Independence.

Dillon and his colleagues were enraged at what they saw as the criminal stupidity and arrogant delinquency of the rebel leaders, but they were also angry at the failure of the British to understand the nuances of the Irish Nationalist political mindset. When he was heckled, his response is perhaps best understood if one remembers that he was first and last an Irishman. The emotional ethnic nerve endings were afire again: 'It would be a damned good thing for you if your soldiers were able to put up as good a fight as did these men in Dublin.' He declared that he was 'proud of their courage, and if you were not so dense and stupid, as some of you English people are, you could have had these men fighting for you'. The MPs in Westminster were outraged, but Dillon went on: 'I say deliberately that in the whole of modern history, taking all the circumstances into account, there has been no rebellion or insurrection put down with so much blood and so much savagery as the recent insurrection in Ireland.'[8]

That this was obviously an exaggeration on Dillon's part only serves to highlight the anger of a man watching his life's work and deep longing for a peaceful transition to Home Rule being swept away by the determination of a very few men prepared to die for their holy cause, in some cases welcoming death, and the response of an Empire outraged by an act of treachery as it fought for its own survival.

*   *   *

In just over two years Dillon, Redmond and the Irish Parliamentary Party were consigned to oblivion by a combination of Irish Nationalist support for the emerging Republican party, Sinn Fein, and more importantly by a ham-fisted attempt by the British government to introduce conscription for Ireland.

That the executions of the rebel leaders produced sympathy for the cause they were designed to crush is beyond doubt. Irish Catholicism was also a major factor. By receiving Holy Communion before he died, Connolly had effectively converted; he'd also almost certainly persuaded his wife to embrace Roman Catholicism. Lillie formally converted on 15 August 1916. 'The fact [was] that in his own lifetime Connolly had been forced to resort to a number of half-truths and occasional outright false representations of his religious position.'[9] Real revolutionaries lie when the cause calls for it, simple as that; Sir Roger Casement also converted to Catholicism before his execution.

Reports of the piety of the rebels, before, during and after the insurrection, were soon in circulation. Masses, Rosaries and prayers now began to celebrate the martyrs' deaths, and religious memorabilia of all kinds eulogised their devotion to faith and fatherland. The *Catholic Bulletin* ran a series of articles called 'Events of Easter Week'. I have read some of them recently and one could be forgiven for thinking all the leaders were candidates for canonisation. A sacred cult that revered death was branded for ever on the Nationalist consciousness. It has stalked Ireland ever since.

Sinn Fein, an organisation that played no part in the Rising, was transformed during the period after it, although it would be several months before it was clear that the party had the ability to respond to its newfound national prominence, or that it was indeed on the cusp of considerable political achievement.

Many of the prisoners released in December 1916 now joined Sinn Fein and this helped give it its sense of a nationwide organisation. The Irish Republican Brotherhood was looking for an existing political party to infiltrate, and Sinn Fein – which owed much of its recent popularity to the efforts of British politicians and the British media who, searching for a handy phrase, dubbed the Rising the 'Sinn Fein Rebellion' – fitted the bill.

Newly energised, Sinn Fein now enjoyed success in a number of parliamentary by-elections in 1917, but so did the Irish Parliamentary Party, which was far from fatally damaged until the attempt by the British government to introduce conscription in April 1918.* The reason for this was the success of the German offensive on the Western Front, which had stunned the British government and was quite possibly the greatest crisis of the war. The government and British public opinion were in no mood to exclude Ireland from conscription in such precarious circumstances.

* In fact, conscription was never implemented in Ireland, but the damage had been done.

Within Ireland an anti-conscription campaign comprising almost every strand of Nationalist opinion and crucially the backing of the Irish Catholic Church attracted overwhelming support. It was the perfect opportunity for Sinn Fein to strengthen its appeal. With its core of 1916 veterans, released prisoners and ageing Fenians, it began to share platforms at public meetings with priests and bishops. Alongside its growing popularity was the reorganisation of the Irish Volunteers, soon to be known as the Irish Republican Army; training drills and raids for arms were becoming commonplace. In the west of Ireland in particular land redistribution had long been a major issue, and both Sinn Fein and the IRA were ever ready to lend a hand. Because of the war emigration was greatly reduced, and land hunger increased support for the militants.

The general election of December 1918 was a resounding success for Sinn Fein in terms of seats gained, even though it took less than half of all votes cast. Sinn Fein won seventy-three seats, the Irish Parliamentary Party a mere six and the Unionists twenty-six. The Irish Labour Party, which owed so much to Connolly, did not contest this election or the one in 1921, having decided to stand aside and let the elections be a plebiscite on Ireland's national future. It is important to remember, however, that this election was fought more on the 'no conscription here' issue than a mandate for an Irish Republic. There were few who claimed that it was a vote for armed revolution.

The newly elected Sinn Fein MPs refused to attend Westminster and set up an alternative parliament, Dail Eireann, in Dublin on 21 January 1919, to which all new Irish MPs were invited. Only the Sinn Fein members accepted the invitation, and of these only twenty-eight were able to attend, the others either being imprisoned, on the run or otherwise occupied. The Dail declared Ireland a Republic, formulated a constitution and appointed delegates to the Paris Peace Conference, which they were not allowed to attend because of the British government's resistance.*

Coincidentally, on the same day what has generally come to be accepted as the first IRA action of the War of Independence took place at Soloheadbeg in County Tipperary. Two members of the Royal Irish Constabulary, who were guarding a convoy of explosives on its way to a local quarry, were shot dead by members of the local IRA. Although not a declaration of war by the Dail, it may well have appeared that way to the British government and media.

The Soloheadbeg ambush was a local initiative by particularly militant IRA volunteers, some of whom would go on to become notorious. One of them, Dan Breen, later said that he felt the IRA volunteers were in great danger of becoming merely a political adjunct to

* One of the hopes of the 1916 leaders was that the Rising would ensure Ireland's attendance at such a conference, which would, they believed, be called by Germany.

Sinn Fein. In other words, the military men would call the shots and, just like the men of 1916, no mandate beyond their will was required to do this.

Throughout 1919 the so-called war stuttered along. By no means did all members of the Dail agree with an armed campaign, believing that the overwhelming support and passive resistance of the Irish people for self-government would win the day. It should also be recorded that many volunteers, who were Catholic and from rural and small-town backgrounds, were initially very reluctant to kill Royal Irish Constabulary men who were themselves mostly Irish and Catholic, and likely to be supporters of Home Rule.

All of this was to change, however. I know from my own experience that for most people killing does not come easy, but the drumbeat becomes louder as the heart darkens, and exposure makes casual brutality all too acceptable. Or, as Richard English puts it: 'Provocation, retaliation and counter-revenge between the opposing sides produced sequences of interlocking reprisals and cycles of violence which – once ignited – could prove nastily self-fuelling.'[10]

The details of the War of Independence have been recorded and interpreted by people much better qualified for the job than I am. It was bloody, squalid and at times, particularly in areas like West Cork (perhaps the IRA's most effective area), undoubtedly sectarian as Unionists were intimidated, sometimes murdered and their houses and businesses burned down. There is no suggestion that these loathsome deeds were directed or sanctioned by the Dail, but they did lay bare an ugly reality: hatred of Unionists and the Protestant 'planter' is buried deep in the dark recesses of extreme Irish Nationalism.

In July 1921 a truce was arranged between the IRA and the Crown. Even at this stage the forces of Sinn Fein and the IRA represented a broad front, stretching from people who had been fervent supporters of Home Rule and were more than ambivalent about the use of violence, to those who would settle for nothing less than a united Irish Republic as laid down by the martyrs of 1916. It also included those who had fallen in love with a lifestyle of conflict and were addicted to power, which had become an end in itself. There was also a sprinkling of Connollyites who were committed to a workers' republic.

Eventually negotiations took place in London, which led to the signing of the Anglo-Irish Treaty on 6 December 1921. The deal offered twenty-six of Ireland's counties qualified autonomy: an Irish Free State with dominion status membership of the British Commonwealth; a British naval presence in three Irish ports; the creation of the post of a governor-general; and an oath of fealty to the Crown (not an oath of allegiance, as is sometimes claimed).

Six counties of Northern Ireland were excluded, and were to remain part of the United Kingdom provided for in the Government of Ireland Act 1920.* Crucially for

---

* Northern Ireland therefore existed prior to the Treaty negotiations.

many Northern Ireland Nationalists who supported it, the Treaty included provision for a Boundary Commission which would go on to examine the future composition of Northern Ireland. Nationalists held out great hope that this commission would hand over large swathes of Northern Ireland to the Irish Free State, but they were to be disappointed.

This was most certainly not the Republic most had envisioned, and though it certainly delivered more than the Home Rule Act postponed from 1914, whether it could justify the violence, bitterness and deaths of the inter-vening years is still a matter of serious dispute.

On 7 January 1922 the Dail agreed by sixty-four votes to fifty-seven to accept the Treaty, but Nationalist Ireland was split and riven at every level. Michael Collins, himself a veteran of the Rising and the IRA's most charismatic leader and fervent advocate of the Treaty, argued that it was the best deal available, declaring that it gave them 'freedom, not the ultimate freedom, that all nations desire and develop to, but the freedom to achieve it'.[11]

A general election took place on 16 June 1922 and recorded an emphatic majority in favour of the Treaty. The Irish Labour Party contested it and won seventeen seats. However, many of the IRA's best-known leaders and a large section – led by Eamon de Valera, another 1916 leader who had been sentenced to death but reprieved – refused to accept the will of the people.

Previous to this, on 14 April 1922, a group of IRA men

had occupied the Four Courts and other buildings in central Dublin in defiance of the new Free State government and even some of their own leaders, who they locked out. This gang regarded themselves as the real defenders of the Republic, and their refusal to renounce it in the face of opposition partly armed and encouraged by the British to my young mind had all of the valour and drama of the Alamo. However, after the June 1922 election, the establishment of a new police service and Free State Army, and under intense pressure from the British government, the Irish Free State had little option but to face its moment of truth.

On 28 June, the occupants of the Four Courts refused a final ultimatum to leave, and the Free State Army launched an assault using artillery borrowed from the British government. But before the rebels surrendered, the Public Record Office, which was part of the Four Courts complex, was destroyed. Fighting was also going on in O'Connell Street, and over £5 million worth of damage was caused.

The resulting Civil War was a vicious and ruthless affair, and the Free State Army, ably led by Michael Collins and his staff and rich in resources compared to its opponents, was far superior in every military judgement. Atrocities were carried out on both sides but what is clear is that except for pockets in the south and west of Ireland, the Irish Free State government enjoyed the support of the general population. The Catholic Church was also firmly on the side of the new government, which denounced the anti-Treaty IRA and excommunicated its members.

In August 1922 Michael Collins was shot dead in an ambush in his native West Cork, and within two months the government had introduced military courts with the authority to impose the death penalty, which they were not shy about using. 'I am not going to hesitate if the country is to live, and if we have to exterminate 10,000 Republicans, the three million of our people is bigger than this ten thousand,' W.T. Cosgrave stated. Cosgrave, a 1916 veteran, was now president of the Executive Council of the Free State, and therefore quasi-prime minister.[12]

Over the next months dozens of captured Republicans were executed, many of them in Kerry, and for Republicans in Kerry they were the most revered martyrs of all. In May 1923 the anti-Treaty forces effectively surrendered when the order was given to cease fire and dump weapons. The Civil War was over, yet the bitterness would last for years, and the IRA – now illegal and defeated – was still armed and still a force to be reckoned with. William O'Brien and Thomas Johnson, the senior leaders of the labour movement, urged support for the Treaty. Others took the anti-Treaty side, among them three of Connolly's children and Constance Markievicz. It is difficult in the extreme to believe that Connolly would have supported the Treaty.

*　　*　　*

Looking at the period after the Rising it is clear that Connolly's influence had been marginalised, sometimes by design and sometimes simply by the force and urgency of events. The Catholic Church was extremely proactive in smothering any mention of socialism, and was content to let Pearse and his vision of Ireland be sanctified. The labour movement was wary of being identified as extreme socialist or Nationalist, and most IRA members had no socialist inclinations.

Pearse and Connolly were the two giants of the 1916 rebellion, but it was now Pearse who had the most defining influence on the politics of the Rising, the immediate legacy of which did not include a socialist or Marxist dimension. But during more recent years, and slowly at first, the Connolly legacy has grown in influence and Pearse has been perceived as a deeply troubled child-man with a messianic view of himself, a martyr complex and an infantile view of the world.

Today, Connolly's legacy is alive and well, his speeches and writings never more relevant in a post-Celtic Tiger Ireland in which people wonder where it all went wrong. Every left-wing and Republican group, violent or otherwise, has adopted Connolly as their patron saint. His name has recently been on the lips of anti-austerity protesters, and at most Sinn Fein and dissident Republican events. The trade unions and the Irish Labour Party have of course always claimed him as their founding father.

Connolly's legacy is that he used his own body and those of the Volunteers in his Irish Citizens Army to forge a socialist Labour alliance with extreme Irish Nationalists. In so doing he sought to make unimportant the more moderate voices within the two. In this he undoubtedly failed, but what he did achieve, as a direct result of his actions, was to make perfectly rational the notion that extreme Irish Nationalists and socialists could work together, using violence, to end British rule in Ireland.

Chapter 7

A REBEL SPIRIT

The Civil War had been deeply traumatic: brother had literally fought brother, and the bitterness poisoned political life and much else in Ireland for generations. The new government of the Irish Free State was also facing huge problems. The numbers for the dead and injured during the Civil War are still not satisfactorily settled, but around 800 government soldiers were killed and many more on the anti-Treaty side.* The Irish government also executed seventy-seven prisoners.

In the latter stages of the Civil War the anti-Treaty campaign degenerated into a wholesale destruction of

* One estimate has it that during the Civil War, which lasted eleven months, six times more Nationalists were killed than those killed by the British forces in the five years between the Rising and the signing of the Treaty.

roads and railway lines, armed robberies, the burning of Protestant-owned houses and an escalation in the murders of Protestants (most prominently in West Cork). The war also became an excuse to settle personal vendettas under the cloak of Republicanism, and murderous disputes over land, particularly in the west of the country, were often settled by whichever IRA leader or faction held control. There is too much evidence available now to dispute the substance of these facts. One of the last acts of the anti-Treaty forces was the burning of two Protestant schools in Cork.

For me, the story of the glorious resistance by Republican heroes, which so informed my childhood years, has become largely a tale of delusion and addiction to a cult of violence. Certainly some men died well during the Civil War, and some fought bravely against hopeless odds, but to my mind they all killed or were killed need-lessly. It should also be said that the new Irish government displayed a ruthlessness to their former comrades-in-arms which no British government of the period could possibly have countenanced. But the new government understood the enemy well, and knew that any hint of compromise or weakness on their part would be punished brutally and without mercy, and then the new state might collapse with hideous consequences.

It can be said of few disputes that one side was totally in the wrong, but in the case of the Civil War, having travelled a long and sometimes bloody road to get where I am today, I have no doubt that the arrogance and contempt for democracy of the anti-Treaty forces and the belief that they alone were the lawful government of Ireland in direct succession from the martyrs of 1916 was wholly responsible for all that followed.

But what was Connolly's legacy in the years immediately after his execution? His son, Roddy, who fought in the Rising, was the first leader of the Communist Party of Ireland and the first leader to oppose the Treaty publicly. He also travelled to Russia twice during this period, and assured Lenin that most of the IRA could be won over to communism.

The simple fact is that there had been little support for Marxism in Ireland before the Rising – witness the minimal backing Connolly received electorally in Dublin – and there was little afterwards. Post-1916 Nationalism, and more specifically Catholic Nationalism, was what it was all about.

The Irish Transport and General Workers Union was also in dire straits after the Rising. Membership had declined steadily during Connolly's period in charge, perhaps because most of its members had no interest in revolution. British Army recruitment during the First World War also accounted for much of the decrease; as we know estimated figures suggest that around 2–3,000 members of the ITGWU enlisted in the British Army during the war.

Even within the Irish Citizen Army, where one might expect to find much of Connolly's teaching reflected, the ideals of its members were broadly similar to their comrades in the Irish Volunteers, especially where religion was concerned. They were different in that they were Dublin-based and many were trade unionists, but for all Connolly's efforts, the ICA was about as distant from the revolutionary Red Guards as the Volunteers were.

This can be observed when Connolly's second-in-command, Michael Mallin, wrote to his wife before his execution: 'My darling Wife Pulse of my heart, this is the end of all things earthly; sentense [*sic*] of Death has been passed, and a [*sic*] quarter to four tomorrow the sentense will be carried out by shooting ... and so must Irishmen pay for trying to make Ireland a free nation.' He goes on to ask his wife to see to it that his youngest son Joseph would become a priest and his daughter Una a nun 'so that we might have two to rest on as penance for our sins ... I do not believe our Blood has been shed in vain,' he writes, and that Ireland 'will come out greater and grander'. He was also adamant that Ireland should not forget that she was Catholic, and must keep her faith.[1] After the Rising the ICA was insignificant and its membership largely swept up by the IRA.

It is pretty clear which vision was going to win out. After the executions, and with the release of union officials such as William O'Brien, reorganisation of the ITGWU began. By late 1917 membership increased quickly to about 12,000, by mid-1918 a union census claimed 44,000 members, and by that year's end the figure was just under 68,000, with some 210 branches. This was almost certainly reflective of the general mood of

Nationalist Ireland. The ITGWU was thriving and was very much in the syndicalist mode of the One Big Union.

In August 1916 the first Irish Trade Union Congress and Labour Party conference since the Rising took place in Sligo. Perhaps inevitably, it was a somewhat confused gathering and failed to take a clear stand on anything. There was certainly no talk of revolution from its senior figures. The president was Thomas Johnson, an English-born Protestant based in Belfast, and it fell to him to make the opening keynote address. Johnson had known Connolly in Belfast and, even though poles apart in temperament and politics, they appear to have at least tolerated each other. Johnson's priority, as he saw it, was to maintain trade union unity, which was no easy task given that north-east Ulster was not only a Unionist stronghold but also had the highest concentration of industrial workers. After praising Connolly he then asked the delegates to remember their colleagues who had died in the First World War and the Rising and, as a measure of respect, to rise for those who had given their lives for a cause they believed in.

Connolly would have been enraged by this request, but Johnson was dealing with reality not sloganising. Ulster was the most industrialised part of Ireland at this time, and the vast majority supported the Union of Ireland and Great Britain. Trying to preserve whatever unity was possible between Nationalist and Unionist workers was the pressing concern of Johnson's leadership. The reality was that Connolly's actions and the Rising itself had only widened already deep divisions.

The ITGWU and much of the Irish labour movement was also going through a period of intense sympathy with and support for the Russian Revolution and the communist government. As William O'Brien said in 1918, when Connolly 'laid down his life for the Irish working class he laid it down for the working class in all countries ... We know the influence it exercised among those great men and women who have given us the Great Russian Revolution.'[2]

It is easy to see why there would be support for the new government of Russia in both Nationalist and Labour circles in Ireland. Sympathy for fellow rebels and a desire to see 'the big fellah' put in his place accounted for much of this. A huge crowd attended a meeting in Dublin in 1918, which was called to congratulate the Russian people on the triumph they had recently won for democratic principles. A platform speaker's call for the Viceregal Lodge in Dublin to be turned into the head office of the ITGWU was loudly applauded.

By 1919 soviets were being established in a number of small towns and villages around Ireland, of which the Limerick Soviet was easily the most important. It was formed after a general strike was called in April, and was commonly known as the 'permit strike' because the military required its citizens to have a permit to move in and out of the town. The Limerick Soviet lasted from 13–24 April, when it effectively collapsed following the intervention of the bishop and mayor, who wrote to the Limerick Trades Council asking that the strike be ended.

'Soviet' was a rather grandiose title for these co-operative or community ventures that reflected the new spirit of freedom, the anti-conscription campaign, the large vote for Sinn Fein and the establishment of the Dail. However, despite attempts then and later by some socialist writers and commentators, this should not, in my view, be interpreted as support among the Irish working-class for Marxism.

Once the Civil War had ended in victory for the Irish Nationalist bourgeoisie they set about creating a state in their likeness. There was no room in their hearts or minds for people like Connolly. They had little in common with Pearse either, for these were practical men who knew that Ireland was not, in the words of Eoin MacNeill, 'a poetical abstraction', but both Church and State used the Pearseian Nationalist Catholic legacy to strengthen the established social, economic and political order they were determined to entrench.

The new Irish Free State was never officially a Catholic state, nor could it have been since the constitution that governed it was based on the Anglo-Irish Treaty of 1921. As Conor Cruise O'Brien states: 'The English Liberals had had to face, ever since Gladstone's conversion to Home Rule in 1886, the Tory argument about Home Rule. Their answer had to be one that became familiar in later decolonisations: that of "built in guarantees" to ensure that the emancipated colony would behave in a manner acceptable to the norms of metropolitan public opinion.'[3]

Neither Northern Ireland nor the Free State could therefore officially endorse any religion. The crucial word here is 'officially', in that both states were nominally secular because the process out of which they had come prevented them from being anything else. In Michael Laffan's words, it should also be remembered that the Civil War 'crippled and poisoned the independent Irish state; it inaugurated a bitter ice age that froze Irish politics for generations'.[4]

The first president of the Executive Council of the Free State, W. T. Cosgrave, had been sentenced to death for his part in the Rising. This was later commuted to life imprisonment, and like most of his fellow veterans he served a very short sentence. Cosgrave was in many respects the archetypal 'grey man', but he was a formidable administrator, a deceptively hard character steeped in obedience to Mother Church.

And Cosgrave was no fool: he knew what he wanted for Ireland, and it was not what his comrade-in-arms James Connolly had wanted. Above all else he desired order; his real challenge was to achieve and maintain it within a democratic framework. And he succeeded. A major factor in this success was the total support from the Irish Catholic Church. In fact, in October 1922 the Irish Catholic hierarchy had declared in favour of the Free State and ordered a general excommunication of any IRA member carrying on the struggle against it.

The sectarian violence in Northern Ireland in the early 1920s was savage and bloody, particularly in Belfast, and no one involved emerged well. To Northern Protestants the IRA in the South often appeared to be engaged in a war against Protestants as well as waging a war against Northern Ireland, and so they took revenge against Northern Catholics, who were not slow to respond. The numbers killed in Belfast alone during 1920–22 reached nearly 500, but there, as in the South of Ireland, the IRA was soundly defeated.

However, the new arrangements slowly settled in. It might be too much to say that they took root, but the new political landscape was taking shape. Yet there was one remaining and potentially destabilising issue. The Anglo-Irish Treaty had provided for a Boundary Commission to examine the newly created Irish border and see if it needed adjusting. It was commonly assumed, certainly by Nationalists, that parts of Northern Ireland close to the border where there was a Nationalist majority would be transferred to Free State authority. The theory was that what was left of Northern Ireland would not then be economically viable, and the Unionists, being 'a hard-headed and sensible people',* would see sense and themselves become Irish Nationalists.

* To most Unionists, this was an intensely patronising and ingratiating phrase beloved of Nationalists.

But when its findings were leaked in November 1925, the Boundary Commission had done no such thing. In fact, it had been decided to leave things much as they were; the detailed findings of the report were not made public until as late as 1969. Before its judgement was due in December 1925, Eoin MacNeill, the man who had countermanded the Rising and was now minister for education in the Free State government, resigned his position as the Irish representative on the Boundary Commission.

The reality of partition was made clear by the muted reaction of many nationalists who, as Michael Laffan states, 'deplored partition [but] felt able to cherish their grievance while at the same time finding the independent state a more congenial place without the presence of a million Ulster Unionists'. He continues: 'Redmond had accepted partition in 1914, and in practice so did the Easter rebels two years later; they planned to launch an insurrection only in the three southern provinces and leave Ulster in peace.'[5] For all of them Ulster was 'different', and had been ever since the plantations.

So Cosgrave and his government got on with the business of establishing and running the new Free State, taking great care, some said too much care, to remain within the terms of the Treaty. IRA violence still threatened, and while Republicans refused to partake in politics and the bitterness from the Civil War permeated everything, future stability could not be taken for granted. However, largely due to the efforts of Cosgrave, the constitutional administrator with nerves of steel and unflinching determination, the Irish Free State slowly evolved into a relatively stable and peaceful democracy. It was an extraordinary achievement.

In 1926 Eamon de Valera* finally faced reality, moving to abandon non-recognition of the Free State and enter its parliament. Most Republicans followed the man they recognised as their chief – including, somewhat surprisingly, Constance Markievicz – and a new party named Fianna Fail was created. A small rump of irreconcilables remained in Sinn Fein.

During this period the Irish Catholic Church was perhaps at its most vocal in its hostility to anything that smacked of godless and foreign creeds. This, in effect, meant anything vaguely left-wing or radical. In Cosgrave it had a tough but compliant ally, and in 1931, worried about the activities of the IRA, and what appeared to be a left-wing drift among Republican organisations in general, as well as the Communist Party of Ireland, he decided to write to the head of the Catholic Church in Ireland asking for its support for new legislation to curb these threats. In his view, only the Roman Catholic Church had the moral authority to alert parents of the dangers to young people of communist and other

---

* It would be 1932 before de Valera finally achieved power with the co-operation of the Irish Labour Party and began the job of dismantling the Treaty and putting in place a new constitution in 1937 that would give a special position to the Catholic Church while claiming jurisdiction over Northern Ireland.

subversive teachings. He also included a document that alleged a conspiracy to overthrow the state by a number of communist groups.

The Church knew what it had to do. On Sunday 18 October a joint pastoral letter was read to every Roman Catholic congregation in Ireland warning the faithful against both the IRA and its socialist offshoot Saor Eire. 'It is our duty,' stated the letter, 'to tell our people plainly that the two organisations to which we have referred, whether separate or in alliance, are sinful and irreligious, and that no Catholic can lawfully be a member of them.' Priests were encouraged to protect young people from the 'satanic tendencies' of communism.[6]

In March 1933 a large crowd of Irish Catholics attacked and looted the headquarters of the Revolutionary Workers' Groups in Dublin. The headquarters was named Connolly House, but being named after Connolly was not enough to save it from a mob fired up on anti-communist rhetoric. The Irish Labour Party was so cowed by this opposition to anything akin to communism, in reality a catch-all phrase for the still active IRA and small groups like Saor Eire, the Republican Congress and the Communist Party of Ireland, that by 1937 the parliamentary leader of the Irish Labour Party, William Norton, signed a letter to the cardinal secretary of state in the Vatican as 'Your Eminence's most humble servant'.

By the time of the Irish Labour Party's annual conference in 1938 the Church effectively demanded that the party change its constitution to remove its commitment to a 'Workers' Republic'. In proposing the motion, Norton said that he understood there would be considerable concern over the matter as some of the delegates would associate the words with the activities of a man whose actions were revered throughout the world. He was, of course, referring to James Connolly. Thus, at the behest of the Irish Catholic Church, the Irish Labour Party and the labour movement in general renounced Connolly's political dream.

The radical Republican left was made of sterner stuff, but, already denounced as communist and subversive, and with scant public support, it had little to lose by sticking to Connolly. Saor Eire and the Republican Congress kept the faith, seeing him as the crucial figure to focus on. It was Connolly's spirit that drove left-wing Republican groups during this period.

However, for all the attention they attracted they were small, ineffectual groups whose power was often hyped by Church and State to prove that there was a serious communist threat in Ireland. The truth is that Ireland was a deeply conservative and largely pious Catholic country, and there was very little support for any kind of radical socialism. Any sympathy for republicanism was mostly corralled by de Valera's Fianna Fail party, which on entering government in 1932 effectively set about dismantling those aspects of the Anglo-Irish Treaty which Republicans and many Irish Nationalists found objectionable.

When the Spanish Civil War broke out in 1936 the Church and respectable Nationalist Ireland rushed to support Franco, not so much to defend fascism as to fight communism and promote Catholicism. A movement which became known as the Blueshirts and had been founded to defend Cumann na nGhael, the pro-Treaty party, from IRA supporters and whose guiding light was the charismatic but erratic Eoin O'Duffy, a former general in the Free State Army, eventually merged with Cumann na nGhael to form Fine Gael.* There is no doubt that, although they were a Catholic Nationalist group, the Blueshirts aped fascist fashion in their wearing of blue shirts and adoption of the straight-arm salute.

Catholic Ireland backed Franco and remained aloof from fighting fascism in the Second World War – and why wouldn't it? The struggle for Irish independence had been fought mainly by a conservative Catholic Ireland, which meant that the Blueshirts were as representative of Irish Nationalism as were the IRA. So when the Spanish Civil War broke out Catholic Ireland and the Blueshirts knew exactly whose side they were on.

'When hundreds of O'Duffyite volunteers set off [to fight for Franco] from the Irish west coast in December 1936, there were bands, hymn-singing crowds and crusade-blessing priests to send them off resoundingly.'[7] And when a small group of Irish Republicans – led by Frank Ryan and composed mainly of ex-members of Saor Eire and the Republican Congress (both of which were

---

* At the time of writing, Fine Gael is still the dominant party in Ireland's coalition government.

now defunct) – as well as some communists left that same month to fight against Franco they almost had to sneak out of the country. Calling themselves the Connolly Column and led by Ryan, they became part of the International Brigades and fought with some distinction in Spain.

To make matters clearer still, Ryan was on record as saying that he wanted a German victory in the Second World War. After being captured in Spain he ended up in Germany as a 'special guest'. He eventually teamed up with 1916 veteran Sean Russell, then the IRA chief of staff, who had travelled there, after a fundraising trip to America, in an abortive attempt to return to Ireland and start a revolt with Nazi help. Russell died on a German U-boat off the west coast of Ireland, and Ryan then returned to Germany where he died in 1942. There is a monument to Sean Russell in Dublin, and Sinn Fein still holds an annual commemoration there to celebrate his role in the struggle for Irish freedom.

Russell was also the driving force behind an IRA bombing campaign in England that began in 1939. The IRA itself was clear where it stood. 'Today England is locked in a life and death struggle with Germany and Italy. From what quarter shall the government of the Irish Republic* seek for aid? The lesson of history is plain. England's enemy is Ireland's ally.'[8]

The bombing campaign in England was a disaster for

---

* The IRA still regarded itself as the legitimate government of Ireland.

the IRA. Many of the big names from the organisation opposed it, and people such as Sean MacBride (son of Maud Gonne) and Tom Barry, the legendary IRA leader in the War of Independence, finally severed their links with it. The campaign and the IRA's high-handed and unpopular activity in Ireland finally forced de Valera to clamp down on the organisation and hundreds of IRA members were interned without trial.* The concern that IRA activity would force Britain to occupy Southern Ireland again would ensure that the government's crackdown could continue throughout the war.

During the Second World War (referred to in Ireland as the Emergency) the country remained neutral. The Irish government executed a number of IRA members, allowed others to die on hunger strike, and went on to claim that it had smashed the IRA, which was undoubtedly at its lowest ebb ever.

And so it was that, without much fanfare, in 1938 something that would have a serious impact on Ireland's future took place in London when a small group of Irish Republicans, radicals and trade unionists came together to form the Connolly Club, later to be renamed the Connolly Association.

---

* Evidence of IRA collaboration with the Nazis came with the capture of a number of German spies in Ireland, as well as with Sean Russell's death. De Valera had real reason to fear that IRA activity might force the British government's hand.

Chapter 8

AFTER THE WAR

On the death of Adolf Hitler in 1945, Eamon de Valera paid a visit to the German ambassador to Ireland and expressed the Irish people's sympathy with the German people. For the British, and indeed the Unionists in Northern Ireland, it must have been extraordinarily insulting and could only be explained by the fact that Eire, the official name of the state following the new constitution introduced by de Valera in 1937, had remained neutral during the war.

Notwithstanding this, as many as 60,000 Southern Irish people had served in the Allied Forces, and many thousands had moved to Britain to find work in the thriving munitions industry. Once again the evidence showed that there was a much more complicated relationship between the Irish and British peoples than the simple Irish

Nationalist narrative of 800 years of British oppression would have one believe.

Before war had broken out, the IRA, now a shadow of its former self after de Valera's embrace of constitutional politics, decided to follow in the footsteps of O'Donovan Rossa and Tom Clarke and carry out a bombing campaign in England. The campaign was the long-held ambition of the IRA's then chief of staff Sean Russell, another veteran of the Rising. On 12 January 1939 the IRA, still believing it was the legitimate government of the Irish republic, delivered an ultimatum to the British government. 'A period of four days is sufficient for your Government to signify its intention in the matter of the military evacuation and for the issue of your declaration of abdication in respect of our country. Our Government reserve the right of appropriate action without further notice if on the expiration of the period of grace, these conditions remain unfulfilled.'[1] If this statement appears delusional or simply mad, that is because it was.

On 16 January 1939 seven bombs exploded in London, Birmingham, Liverpool and Manchester, where a passer-by was killed. By July of that year 145 more bombs had exploded in England. The campaign reached a bloody climax on 25 August when a bomb attached to a bicycle exploded in the centre of Coventry killing five people and injuring more than fifty. The last recorded incident was the discovery of a bomb in Grosvenor Place, London in March 1940. Two Irishmen, Peter Barnes and James McCormack, were later hanged for their part in the attacks.* The newly formed Connolly Association was active in calls for clemency for both men.

Sean Russell belonged to the wing of Irish Republicanism that loathed politics, particularly anything that smelled of communism, and was wedded to violence not just as a means but as an end in itself. The bombing campaign marked a period when the IRA, not long before a political power in Ireland, degenerated into a militarist sect that revered the gun and the bomb. Wallowing in a state of self-imposed martyrdom it departed the centre stage, occasionally shouting from the wings ineffectually as the rest of the world moved on. Not until the outbreak of violence in Northern Ireland in 1969 would it again become a force to be reckoned with.

Against this background and Ireland's neutrality during the war, de Valera's message of condolence on the death of Hitler was regarded by most British people as a calculated insult. However, the reality was that there was an anti-British sentiment common among the Irish during this period, as well as a desire to assert their new-won independence and a fear that their country could split on the issue of neutrality less than twenty years after the Civil War. Many Irish people still regard this

---

* Their bodies would not be returned to Ireland until 1969, and when they were there was a public attack on the then leadership of the IRA by Jimmy Steele, a prominent traditionalist, who accused the organisation of having fallen under the influence of communists. His speech was another marker on the road to the split that led to the formation of the Provisional IRA.

era as de Valera's finest hour, and he was lauded for standing up to British demands and to Churchill in particular.

De Valera's response to the bombing campaign was rather different as he launched a severe crackdown on the IRA. Fianna Fail was much closer to the IRA until the early 1930s and dual membership was not unknown, but entering government in 1932 had forced responsibility on de Valera, and his administration was becoming increasingly irate at repeated challenges to its authority. The bombing campaign and attempts by the IRA to forge an alliance with Germany were impossible to ignore. The fear that Britain might reoccupy Ireland to protect its flank was also all too real.

In 1936 the IRA had again been declared an illegal organisation, but it was the outbreak of war with Germany that really forced the Irish government to crack down hard. After introducing emergency legislation in June 1939, which allowed for internment without trial and special non-jury courts, over 500 IRA suspects were rounded up in a series of raids in the summer of 1940 and interned without trial in the Curragh military camp in County Kildare, among them my father and his elder brother.

De Valera's new constitution had removed many of the clauses of the Free State constitution, such as the oath of fealty and the post of governor general. The three British naval ports (Berehaven, Queenstown, now Cobh, and Lough Swilly) that had been retained by Great Britain under the terms of the Treaty had also been handed back to the Irish state, and many Republicans felt that de Valera, if slowly, was moving in the right direction. All these factors combined to ensure that there was substantial support for his crackdown on his old comrades in the IRA.

Between 1940 and 1946 six IRA men were executed by army firing squad, having been convicted by a military tribunal. Charlie Kerins, from my hometown Tralee, was hanged by a British hangman, borrowed for the occasion in December 1944. Three others were allowed to die on hunger strike in the same period.

Charlie Kerins was a name I came to know well as I was growing up. Executed for the murder of Garda officer Denis O'Brien,* Kerins's death led to defections from Fianna Fail to the local Labour Party in Kerry. It was also partly responsible for the election of Kerins's boyhood friend Dan Spring as TD for the local area. Spring was a member of the Labour Party and a full-time ITGWU official.

Directly across from the Spring family home in Tralee there is a park and memorial dedicated to Kerins. It is not possible to leave the Springs' house without seeing the monument on the other side of the road. In the 1960s a new local authority housing estate in the area was named

---

* O'Brien was one of the hard-line anti-Treaty men who had occupied the Four Courts in Dublin, thus starting the Civil War.

Kerins Park, and the local Gaelic football club* was renamed Kerins O'Rahillys in his honour.

Spring appealed both to Labour voters and to those who would normally vote for Fianna Fail but now refused to do so because of the 'murder' of Kerins, and who couldn't vote for Sinn Fein as it did not contest elections, or refused to take seats if elected as it still regarded the Irish parliament as an illegal assembly.

There was therefore a coalition around Spring that was Labour, Nationalist and Catholic. He was regarded as sound or supportive on issues such as the release of Republican prisoners, support for the hunger strikers and the North in general. He was always careful to keep this coalition intact, belonging as he did to the conservative wing of Irish Labour. Of course, no speech of his was complete without a few words of praise for Connolly, but it was a Connolly who bore no recognition to the words or writings of the man himself. The family bookshelves were reportedly groaning under the weight of Connolly's writings, but it is doubtful that Spring troubled them very much.

His son Dick went on to take his father's seat, becoming

---

* The club had originally been called after the head of the O'Rahilly clan from County Kerry who was shot dead during the Rising. O'Rahilly had spent the hours before the Rising driving throughout the South of the country urging volunteers to obey MacNeill's countermanding order. On returning to Dublin and realising the Rising was happening anyway, he decided to take part, saying to Constance Markievicz, 'It is madness but it is glorious madness.'

leader of the Labour Party and Tánaiste (deputy prime minister). He also played a positive role in the process that eventually led to the Belfast Agreement. But he too had to pay attention to his base, once holding onto his seat by four votes when he was deemed to be insufficiently sound on the current issues in the North. He eventually lost his seat to Martin Ferris of Sinn Fein, who was, of course, especially sound on 'The North'.

This was the tradition I was born into, an anti-state, anti-Establishment, militarist tradition. Owing more to the Civil War, it had a fierce anti-politician, anti-clerical ethos. Some of the members of the sect, for sect it was, enjoyed a certain respect in the area. They were regarded as 'men of honour' with a rough integrity and who had held fast to their ideals, even though most of them were hopelessly deluded. They would be called upon occasionally to sort out local disputes, usually relating to issues over land.

To see how Irish neutrality and Irish Nationalism were viewed in Britain during and immediately after the Second World War and particularly in the British labour movement, one could do worse than look at what George Orwell had to say.

In a review of Sean O'Casey's autobiography, published in the *Observer* in 1945, Orwell wrote: 'Why is it that the worst extremes of jingoism and racialism have to be tolerated when they come from an Irishman?' He went on to say that, 'Eire was a sham independent state ... hiding behind Britain's protection.' And there was more in the same vein: 'Catholics in England, the bulk of them very poor Irish labourers, were the only really conscious, logical intelligent enemies that democracy has got in England ... They were a silent drag on Labour Party policy but are not sufficiently under the thumb of their priests to be fascist in sympathy.' Orwell described the 1916 Rising as 'a crime and a mistake'. He also believed that the dispute over Ulster was caused by 'the expansionist racist nature of modern Republicanism'.[2]

He had a lifelong antipathy to Catholicism, and Catholic Ireland's neutrality during the Second World War confirmed his prejudice. Having fought on the Republican side in the Spanish Civil War, he was well aware of the Irish Catholic Church's support for Franco, as well as the Blueshirts' role in Spain.

Comparisons were increasingly being made between Irish neutrality during the war and 'loyal Ulster'. In a VE Day radio broadcast Churchill made his views clear: 'The approaches which the southern Irish ports and airfields could so easily have guarded were closed by the hostile aircraft and U-boats. This indeed was a deadly moment in our life, and if it had not been for the loyalty and friendship of Northern Ireland, we should have been forced to come to close quarters with Mr. De Valera, or perish from the earth.'

There was a general feeling that Great Britain had been let down by the Irish, and the British public and the Labour and Conservative Parties valued the Ulster Unionists highly in comparison. This feeling was compounded by many incidents: during the war German spies were arrested in Southern Ireland in the company of IRA sympathisers; in Belfast IRA supporters were known to switch on lights during the blackouts to guide German bombers to the city; the IRA had bombed English cities and towns before and during the early months of the war; its chief of staff died on board a German U-boat; and IRA man Tom Williams was executed on 2 September 1942 for the murder of a policeman in Belfast earlier that year. Is it really any wonder that many British people felt angry with Irish Nationalists?

The years after the Second World War saw an influx of Irish workers to Britain as reconstruction got under way.

The Connolly Club, an organisation founded by several members of the Republican Congress and various individuals from Irish Nationalist and socialist groups, had come together in Doughty Street, London, in 1938 to promote the ideals of their hero. So while the ultra-Nationalist IRA was trying to bomb Britain, supporters of Connolly were organising campaigns to free Republicans who had been taken prisoner in Spain, persuading Irish emigrant workers to join British trade unions, dealing with social issues among the newly arrived Irish, and promoting a general anti-fascist line with regard to events in Europe.

During the war the Association's newspaper, then called *Irish Freedom*, had a large circulation primarily because of the absence of Irish newspapers during this period. In 1941 Charles Desmond Greaves, a lifelong member of the Communist Party of Great Britain, joined, and in 1943 the organisation changed its name to the Connolly Association. While never having more than a few hundred members and a couple of full-time staff it quickly developed a method of operating that ensured it punched well above its weight in terms of political influence.

The general election in Ireland in 1948 saw the end of sixteen years of de Valera and his Fianna Fail government. The new government was a coalition of Fine Gael, a new party called Clann na Poblachta made up of Republicans and socialists, and a witches' brew of independents. It was a most unlikely administration, and its establishment owed much to a shared desire to get rid of de Valera, often for contradictory reasons. The leader of Clann na Poblachta was none other than Sean MacBride, the son of Maud Gonne, James Connolly's old sidekick from the early years of the 1900s.

The new government decided that Ireland, or the 26-county part of it they were responsible for, should leave the Commonwealth and declare itself a Republic. The Taoiseach, John A. Costello, announced this to great surprise on a visit to Canada. The British government immediately responded with the Ireland Act of 1949, which stated that there would be no change in the constitutional position of Northern Ireland without the agreement of the parliament in Stormont.

The Ireland Act gave rise to a great wave of

indignation in Nationalist Ireland as it appeared to re-inforce partition. Some commentators have claimed that the Ireland Act helped to re-energise the IRA, but to what extent is hard to quantify. Meanwhile, the Connolly Association, now firmly under the control of Greaves, was expanding. Branches were formed in Manchester, Liverpool, Northampton and other towns and cities and a veritable blizzard of pamphlets poured forth. Greaves had given up a well-paid job and was now full-time editor of the Association's paper, and much else besides, being regularly described from 1942 on as the 'Communist Party's expert on Ireland'.

But the Connolly Association had a problem: how might it swing the British labour movement around to a more sympathetic view of Irish Nationalism? Entryism – some would call it subversion–* was the answer.

Because of the Connolly Association's relationship with the Communist Party, Special Branch and MI5 kept a close eye on it during this period, as detailed by Matt Treacy in his book *The Communist Party of Ireland, 1921-2011*. This relationship sometimes created tension when new members who thought they had joined a left-wing Republican organisation found that another organisation, and a communist one at that, was also involved. Special Branch was aware of this tension and

* See Sean Redmond's address at the Desmond Greaves Summer School, Dublin, 2005.

penned a note to the effect that Greaves's close connection with the Communist Party was not looked on with favour by some members of the Connolly Association.[3] Greaves's influence on the Connolly Association was thus weakened for a short period at the end of the war, though Special Branch noted that he was remaining 'in obedience to Communist Party instructions'. As Treacy shows, there are copious records of Special Branch accounts of the relationship between the Communist Party of Great Britain and the Connolly Association in the public records in Colindale, which make clear that the relationship between the two was a significant one.

The Connolly Association was also a point of contact with the Irish working class in Great Britain who, because of their Catholicism, were generally hostile to anything that smacked of godless communism. Greaves in particular held firmly to the party line, which often involved having to present more than two faces at any one time. In fact, Irish labourers in the 1950s and 1960s, and sometimes later, were frequently not members of any union and more often employed by Irish sub-contractors who paid them in cash. This sometimes led to British workers refusing to work with them and even going on strike. On at least one occasion the Connolly Association was called on to solve the problem.

The common thread in all this was the promotion of the ideals of James Connolly. These ideals inspired the Irish Communist Party, Saor Eire, the Republican

Congress, the Irish Labour Party, the ITGWU, a dozen other variants of all these, and, of course, the Connolly Association.

In the early 1950s the *Irish Democrat*, with Greaves as editor, began to promote the idea of some sort of civil rights movement in Northern Ireland. Civil rights in Northern Ireland, or rather the perceived lack of them for Catholics, was identified as a major weakness for the Unionist government there. Greaves is credited by many serious students of the period with being the progenitor of the northern civil rights movement.

Greaves and the Connolly Association were not solely responsible for the civil rights movement, but they did play a key role. Their long and often solitary campaign undoubtedly helped pave the way within the British trade union and labour movement for more wide-scale support. Indeed Greaves organised marches in England demanding civil rights for Northern Ireland Catholics before there were marches in Northern Ireland.

It would be a waste of time and paper to even begin to describe the incestuous and squabbling world of what passed for the Marxist left in Ireland during this period. What is clear though is that the Communist Party of Great Britain had a sometimes fractious relationship with the Communist Activists in Ireland because it wanted a good as possible relationship with the Irish government which was not a member of NATO or the then EU. The Communist Party of Great Britain was, however, always interested in the Republican movement, and was careful not to criticise the IRA, some of whose members and supporters it regarded as potentially useful. Greaves was their Irish expert and leading light of the Connolly Association, which was the vehicle through which Irish working-class emigrants could be introduced.

Crucially, the Communist Party of Great Britain recognised that the British Parliament held jurisdiction over Northern Ireland, and that its own powerful influence in the British labour movement meant it could play a major role in exposing what it believed were civil rights abuses being perpetuated by the parliament in Stormont, Northern Ireland. In other words, it wanted to beat up Stormont by challenging it with British democracy. Enough is now known about Soviet communism to realise that this was a totally cynical exercise. The fact was, though, that the Communist Party and the Connolly Association were influential in both the early stages of the formation of the Northern Ireland Civil Rights Association as well as the radicalisation of the Republican movement from the early 1960s onwards.

In the Ireland of the 1950s Connolly was sidelined. I was born in 1954 and must have been about eight or nine when I first became aware of the IRA. I was going to Mass with my father in Tralee when I saw the words 'Join the IRA and Free the Prisoners' painted in large letters on a number of walls. They were new and so they caught my attention, as did my father's reaction, which was one of support for the slogans. It is a fading memory now yet still clear. The graffiti remained for many years until they too faded with age.

When I was eight the IRA Border Campaign, which lasted from 1956 to 1962, ended in what hardly amounted to a whimper. It had been a disaster, and by the end of 1962 the IRA was at a very low ebb. Many members were in jail in Northern and Southern Ireland.

In its early days the Border Campaign had led to a brief emotional revival of militant Republicanism. The deaths of IRA volunteers Sean South from Limerick and Fergal O'Hanlon from Monaghan, in an attack on Brookeborough RUC station in County Fermanagh on New Year's Day 1957, set the scene for a huge outpouring of Nationalist sympathy, with the funerals as usual taking centre stage. Four Sinn Fein members were elected as TDs but, as ever, did not take their seats, and two Sinn Fein MPs were elected in Northern Ireland.

It also gave rise to a number of songs which are often still sung when Irish people gather. Late last year I was walking down a street in East London early one morning after meeting with some young people who hang around the edges of the street gangs in the area, and I became aware that the words of a song from that period – 'The Patriot Game', written by a brother of Brendan Behan – were going around in my head.

They told me how Connolly was shot in a chair,
His wounds from the battle all bloody and bare.

*   *   *

Sympathy for the Border Campaign quickly melted away as both governments began to round up IRA activists and, using their respective Emergency legislations, interned them without charge or trial. It was not necessary to use the British Army in Northern Ireland because the police and their part-time reserves, known as the B Specials, were more than capable of dealing with the problem. The Irish police and army were also active on the Southern side of the border, and effectively and quietly co-operated with their counterparts in the North.

De Valera was finally replaced as Taoiseach by Sean Lemass, himself a 1916 veteran, whose brother had been shot dead by government forces at the end of the Civil War. Lemass's immediate task was to open up the moribund Irish economy to outside investment, and this he began to do with the help of the very capable and far-seeing T.K. Whitaker, governor of the Irish Central Bank.

And so it was that, as the 1950s drew to a close and the long shadow cast by the austere de Valera began to fade, Ireland found itself on the edge of major change.

Chapter 9

MODERNISATION

Sean Lemass had waited a long time to get his hands on the levers of power. Above all else he was keen to end de Valera's policies of economic self-sufficiency and protectionism. Combined with cultural isolationalism, obedience to the Catholic hierarchy and a search for a Gaelic utopia that had never existed, these policies had brought Ireland to its knees. It was a country for old men, with a crumbling infrastructure that survived simply by exporting its young, mainly to Britain.

Lemass, who as a young man in jail in the 1920s could often be found on his own reading books on economic theory, tore up this pecuniary suicide note and invited foreign investment into the country. It was the single internal event that made everything else possible.

The launch of Ireland's first television service, Telefis Eireann, on New Year's Eve 1961 also changed the face of the Irish Republic. On its opening night Lemass 'stressed the central importance of television in opening out Ireland to the world'. De Valera welcomed the arrival of RTE, as it was known, but warned it could if handled wrongly lead to 'decadence and dissolution'.[1]

The Second Vatican Council, which sat between October 1962 and December 1965, also had a major impact on the way Irish people viewed the place of the Church within their lives. I was eleven at the time and have no recollection of the details of the Vatican's deliberations or decisions, but there seemed to be a general perception that the Church was changing and becoming less authoritarian. This was welcomed by some, and not by others, but the tide was with the liberals. My memories are based more on scraps of overheard conversations and arguments, though by then I was regularly reading newspapers that were packed with these issues in a way that is inconceivable now. What is true is that it was now possible to equate Catholicism with social justice in Ireland and the notion of Christian socialism began to feature in public debate.

The visit of John F. Kennedy to Ireland in June 1963 instilled a sense of the Irish Republic being a proper country in its own right. RTE captured scenes of national joy and celebration as Kennedy moved among and spoke to enthusiastic crowds. The first Irish-American Catholic president of the United States had come home! Kennedy's visit also increased hopes of greater American investment in Ireland, and I remember bits of it very well. In what seems to me now an altogether more innocent age, there was a huge sense of unadulterated ethnic pride.

The publication in 1961 of Desmond Greaves's biography of Connolly was also an important occasion, though obviously not on the scale of these other events. Initially Greaves's book was anathema to reactionary Nationalists because it proved beyond doubt that Connolly was not born in Ireland and that he served in the British Army. It also proved conclusively that Connolly was a Marxist and not some fuzzy type of Irish Catholic socialist.

For the most part this hardly seemed to matter. Aside from Nationalists of the most extreme kind, no one really cared where Connolly was born, particularly as his parents were Irish. He was part of the Irish diaspora, and as for his time in the British Army, well, very few people were in a position to throw stones about that without hitting a relative or ancestor. He was simply another Irishman among the hundreds of thousands who had served with the British Forces.

As I write about this period now I can see that it was a chapter of great change, but at the time we were aware of this only dimly. Even though RTE brought these great events into our living rooms, still on summer holidays, along with friends, mornings could be spent going to the creamery with a farmer who passed by our estate with his horse and cart and one or two milk churns. Horse and carts were far from an uncommon sight in those days.

* * *

The IRA Border Campaign ended in 1962, and I was certainly aware of this, but we lived as far from Northern Ireland as it was possible to be and still remain on the island. For me, the IRA were Robin Hood-types and romantic, anti–Establishment figures. I had also read the books: Dan Breen's *My Fight for Irish Freedom*, Tom Barry's *Guerrilla Days in Ireland*, *Kerry's Fighting Story* and a dozen others. And there is one incident in 1960, when I was six, that sticks in my mind. The government had sent two battalions of the Irish Army to the Congo as part of a UN peace-keeping mission; nine men were killed when they were ambushed on 8 November. Over the next couple of years I recall arguments with pals in which I would say they had died for nothing, that the IRA were the real army of Ireland and the dead men should have been fighting with them to free our country – childish spats that demonstrate my inherited skewed view of the world.

After the end of the Border Campaign many Republicans were pretty demoralised. Some drifted away while others, happy to keep the flame alive, fought for the release of prisoners and waited hopefully for the next, and this time successful, campaign to begin.

A small number of Republicans such as Dubliner Cathal Goulding began to question where they were going from here. Goulding had spent the IRA Border Campaign in jail in England, having been caught after a raid for arms at an army depot in Felstead, Essex. Now he and others began to take tentative steps to assess the future role of

Republicanism after years of isolation, delusion and abject failure.

An outgoing and gregarious character, Goulding came from a family steeped in militant Republicanism. A house painter by trade, and a boyhood friend of Brendan Behan, his Dublin working-class roots and general instinct positioned him on the left of the IRA. He had also come to feel that in the past the IRA had been elitist, its attitude towards the masses being more one of, 'We didn't care what these bastards want, we know what is good for them.'[2]

Goulding had been influenced by the Republican Congress of the 1930s, some of whose former members were the driving force behind the formation of the first Connolly Club in 1938. He was also by nature and political instinct a Connolly man rather than a Pearse man. Yet the actual Connolly – the Marxist rather than the Nationalist and Catholic – was not always popular within the IRA, which at the time remained a small, insular, militarist organisation that worshipped violence and martyrdom. An example of this can be seen in the early 1960s in Crumlin Road prison in Belfast when Leo McCormack lectured fellow inmates on Connolly's socialist ideas, causing near violent argument and dissent among some of the prisoners present.

It was this core group, centred on Goulding, who would embrace the ideas and ideologies of Connolly, while looking for inspiration to national liberation movements across the world, from Vietnam to Cuba.

Meanwhile in Ireland, and for the first time in living memory, emigration was dropping, and some people were even coming home. American multinational companies had dramatically increased their investment in Europe, and Ireland began to benefit from this. The draconian censorship laws that banned the works of Irish and international writers also began to be relaxed.

Goulding and the people around him were not having it all their own way, however. Many Sinn Fein and IRA members were fiercely anti-communist, and some speculated that Goulding had been converted by the communist spy Klaus Fuchs while in jail in England. The truth was much simpler. Goulding was a natural left-winger who drew his inspiration from Wolfe Tone, James Connolly and the Republican Congress, and who believed that the great mistake of the Congress was to split from the IRA. Brian Hanley and Scott Millar claim Goulding believed that had the socialists stayed inside the Congress, they could have eventually won over the majority of the IRA.[3]

Goulding and his close associates were radical progressives in the context and history of Ireland at that time. They began to set up discussion groups within and on the fringes of Dublin's Republican and socialist enclaves. Two important people now entered the scene. Roy Johnston and Anthony Coughlan were former members of the Connolly Association who returned to Ireland from England in the early 1960s and became involved in these groups. Johnston was also a member of the Communist Party of Great Britain, and it seems that his membership continued for quite a while after he returned. Some people say that Coughlan was also a member, but he strongly denies this, and there is no proof that he was. He was undoubtedly very close to Greaves and continues to champion him to this day.

Both men began to exert a considerable influence within the Republican movement and no small amount of controversy, especially as it seemed to some of the other, more conservative, long-serving and respected members that they also had an undue effect on Goulding. Meanwhile, out in the country, what was left of the IRA was still waiting for the next campaign to start. Goulding and his colleagues were looking to Castro and Che Guevara, who had toppled Batista in Cuba and were standing up to America – and unlike the Irish revolutionary heroes these guys were successful. At this time, the American civil rights movement was also making headlines around the world.

Greaves was still in charge of the Irish section of the Communist Party of Great Britain, as well as the dominant influence in the Connolly Association. He visited Ireland regularly during this period, and it was Johnston he primarily came to see, though he also met with Goulding, other Republicans and Irish communists, particularly Betty Sinclair in Belfast.

During this time there was also widespread concern about the levels of foreign investment in the country. Sinn Fein stood out against it, believing that Ireland was being sold out to foreign capital and that the Gaelic culture would be swamped. The language in particular was a big issue in that it was perceived as a defining part of Ireland's soul and, although it could no longer be described as a 'living' language, this did not stop some from trying to revive it as such. For instance, it was still not possible to get into university, the civil service or the police service without passing entrance exams in Gaelic. There was therefore a self-serving reason among the professional classes to learn enough Gaelic for the purpose, and then perhaps never use it again. It also meant that the poorer working classes had very little incentive to learn Gaelic because these particular careers had hitherto been closed to them.

In 1948, de Valera had said that, just as France was France without Alsace-Lorraine, so 'Ireland could still be Ireland without the North', but to many the loss of the Gaelic language meant a loss of nationhood at a much deeper level. Hence throughout the 1950s and 1960s we had concerted, expensive and often harsh attempts to revive Gaelic as a living language. I remember at primary school how Israel was praised for its success in reviving Hebrew, for making the desert bloom and, of course, for its violent and successful campaign against British rule. Israel was held up to us as the great example for Ireland to emulate, with little or no mention of its Jewish centrality.

Connolly supported all aspects of Gaelic revival, including the language, but it never exercised him the way it did his peers. It was simply not a priority for him.

He thought that the ability to speak one's own language was essential to a country's sense of its identity, but he was also an enthusiastic supporter of Esperanto as a universal language.

Personally, like many others of my generation, I had a fierce resentment against the obligatory learning of the Irish language. It was just part of the old, reactionary Establishment, and I wanted rid of ALL of that.

Meanwhile, Cathal Goulding, Sean Garland* and Johnston were busy trying to drag their fellow Republicans towards some recognition of reality, the most basic being that the Irish Republic was a living, breathing entity and a legitimate government recognised as such by its citizens, as well as internationally. It was not easy; and, in the light of what they were attempting to do, perhaps they felt that Connolly was too controversial a figurehead. Instead they settled on Wolfe Tone, the Protestant leader of the United Irishmen, who was captured and committed suicide after returning to Ireland with French military assistance in 1798.

By 1963 Wolfe Tone Societies were being set up following the bicentenary of his birth. By far the most important was established in Dublin in 1964 and served as a debating society and a talent-spotting and recruitment hub generally for those of a socialist Republican bent. Roy Johnston had first come into contact with Greaves

* A veteran of the Brookeborough raid that gave rise to the song 'The Patriot Game'.

when a student at Trinity College Dublin in 1953, and they got to know each other quite well when Johnston moved to England and joined the Connolly Association. They did not always see eye to eye, either personally or politically, with Greaves sometimes referring to Johnston as 'useless' and 'lazy'. Nevertheless, before long Johnston had the ear of the IRA leadership and was put in charge of political education, largely at Goulding's insistence.

As one LSE-educated comrade of Goulding's observed: 'Cathal was a Marxist: that was one of the things that didn't endear him to many people … He was very much a man of his times: the 1960s was that burgeoning period, it seemed as if the left was going to sweep the world in front of it.'[4]

Growing up in this period, I remember regarding all the old Nationalist guff, the language, the religion, the piety, the deference and the obvious censorship as hopelessly old-fashioned and part of an order that frankly both embarrassed and disgusted me. Much of it could be summed up in one incident in Tralee in 1967. Jayne Mansfield, the B-list actress and sex siren, was booked to do a show in a nearby hotel. The local parish priest objected. From the pulpit he warned everyone young and old 'to dissociate themselves from this attempt to besmirch the name of our town for the sake of filthy gain'.[5] Her appearance was cancelled. Such was the reality of life in Kerry in 1967 when the Church cracked the whip.

Gaelic games were different. I loved sport but my eyes

were far more inclined to stray to England and English soccer teams. It was still a fact of life that Gaelic footballers or hurlers could be banned from playing for life just for attending a 'foreign' game, such as rugby. Foreign, in sporting terms, meant British; basketball, an American game, however, was very popular in my area and was favoured by lots of Gaelic players both for recreation and fitness.

I would also sometimes read the IRA paper *the United Irishman*, which had an air of danger and mystique, and was now beginning to contain more articles about socialism. Also prominent were reports of protests over poor housing conditions in Dublin and other towns and cities, and campaigns against privately owned fishing rights – usually held by British absentee landlords – along with the reports of IRA commemorations and eulogies for so-called martyrs. It was all a bit of a jumble, and what remains important for me today is the subliminal evaluation of what was new and what was old, along with a craving to be on the 'modern' side.

I am not trying to pretend that at the age of ten or eleven I had a great caught up in or knowledge of politics; I was far more interested in playing soccer and following my favourite English football team, Tottenham, who I still support. I was just railing against the established order. I still think that most youngsters worth their salt should be doing the same.

I was growing up on a council estate built the year I was born, on the edge of a small town with countryside all around. We walked or ran to school on our own, had our dinner at lunchtime and pretty much amused ourselves the rest of the time. There was no immediate sense of the world changing around us, although I was drawn to the local library and read widely. My most vivid memory of the period was that it was dull, and that I wanted to go away somewhere – anywhere, as long as it was away. Where I grew up, having 'ideas above your station' was something to be corrected rather than encouraged.

Northern Ireland was a place we knew little about, heard little about, and as a consequence hardly cared about, except that somehow it was ours. Aside from a few martyr-induced highs, the IRA had limited support from Nationalists north or south of the border. Successive Irish governments had also shown a general desire to crack down hard on IRA activities, which if nothing else should have made it clear to Unionists that the ending of partition was not, in reality, a driving imperative in the daily lives of Irish Nationalists on either side of the border. However, the rhetoric from politicians and other public figures often said the North was ours and we would one day reclaim it. Unionists heard that loud and clear.

In 1964, however, there was a reminder that under the surface in Northern Ireland old atavistic feelings still lurked. I was almost ten years old when the Divis Street riots erupted in Belfast during the British general election. Many commentators now credit it with raising sectarian tension in the North. Perhaps more importantly they also point to it as the arrival of Ian Paisley on the public scene, although he had been a growing force in Northern Ireland politics for some time.

The Republicans who were contesting the election, on an abstentionist basis, decided to place an Irish tricolour flag in the window of a shop in Divis Street, which was acting as their temporary headquarters, even though it was illegal to fly the tricolour in Northern Ireland. Ian Paisley objected and said that if the police refused to remove it he would take the law into his own hands.

The police removed the offending tricolour and, predictably, there was trouble: rioting and demonstrations took place over several days. Though confined to the Divis Street and Falls Road areas, they were probably the most intense riots Belfast had seen in thirty years, and were encouraged by James Connolly's daughter, Ina, who told the demonstrators that their cause was her father's cause.

On 14 January 1965 Captain Terence O'Neill, who had replaced Lord Brookeborough as prime minister of Northern Ireland, invited his Southern counterpart, Sean Lemass, to visit him at Stormont to discuss 'possibilities of practical co-operation in economic matters of mutual interest'. It was a controversial move, prompting Lemass to comment afterwards that things would never be the same again. When he also predicted that he would get into trouble for agreeing to the meeting, O'Neill contradicted him: 'It is I who will get into trouble over this,' he said – as indeed was to be the case.[6]

In fact, O'Neill had been reassured by both the new direction and pragmatism of Lemass, and the quiet but effective co-operation against the IRA during the Border Campaign, and by the decision of the Nationalists in Northern Ireland to refuse to support it. The real problem at the time and throughout the second half of the 20th century was that much of the cause of the civil unrest in the North was never just about relations with the Catholic South, but much more about inter-community relations within Northern Ireland itself.

Republicans in the South were meanwhile engaged in their own machinations. As more of the old traditionalists faded away the IRA took on an increasingly left-wing orientation. The Wolfe Tone Society was a powerhouse for ideas and debate, and the two former members of the Connolly Association were right at the heart of it, while Greaves was never far away.

In May 1965 Greaves's cherished idea of a Northern Ireland Civil Rights Association almost came to fruition at a meeting of the Amalgamated Transport and General Workers Union in Belfast. It was attended by members of various unions, Republicans, Irish Communist's and other interested bodies. Much to the regret of Greaves, who favoured a slow, methodical approach based on putting pressure on Westminster to force change in Northern Ireland, it failed to reach a consensus.

Communists were banned from membership of the Republican movement, so plans for an alliance under the banner of a national freedom movement were taken very gingerly indeed. A good example of the tensions between them was when Betty Sinclair was invited by Goulding to address a Republican rally in Casement Park in Belfast. Local Republicans persuaded the owners of the stadium, the Gaelic Athletic Association, to refuse her permission to speak because she was a communist.

Greaves believed that a civil rights movement in Northern Ireland should be built patiently through trade unions and the labour movement. However, the Northern Ireland Civil Rights Association that eventually came into being in 1967 developed in a quite different way, prioritising marches and street protests modelled on the American civil rights marches.

The big difference, though, was that black people in America were not fighting over sovereignty; there was no 'foreign power' for them to remove, no national territory to unite, or union to defend. In Northern Ireland, on the other hand, civil rights marchers sang 'We shall overcome' while carrying the Irish tricolour, and known IRA men often stewarded the protests. Indeed, as the civil rights movement developed, it became impossible to disentangle ethnic hatred and rage from the legitimate peaceful pursuit of civil rights for Northern Irish Nationalists. Many Ulster Unionists simply saw the movement as the IRA in another guise and reacted as they had done for generations.

Initially the civil rights movement was a broad coalition of Nationalists within Northern Ireland, the Republican left, the Connolly Association, the Communist Party of Great Britain, the Wolfe Tone Societies, trade union activists and various civil liberty groups in England and Ireland. Gerry Fitt was elected as a Republican Labour MP for West Belfast in 1966, and spoke regularly at Connolly Association meetings and helped to brief Labour politicians at Westminster.* He was always a fiercely outspoken critic of the Provisional IRA, and was forced to leave his home after the 1981 hunger strikes.

The Campaign for Social Justice, founded by Conn and Patricia McCluskey in January 1964, was also pivotal to the emerging civil rights movement in Northern Ireland. Small, educated and middle-class, the Campaign for Social Justice concentrated on trying to influence public opinion in England, particularly within the Labour Party, and with some success, it has to be said. I now believe that Northern Ireland never was the South African-type 'apartheid state' it is often portrayed as today.

John Hewitt, the Ulster Marxist poet and one-time member of the Connolly Association, says it best for me.

> You coasted along.
> And all the time, though you never noticed,
> The old lies festered;
> The ignorant became more thoroughly infected;
> There were gains, of course;
> You never saw any go barefoot.
> ... You coasted along.
>
> From 'The Coasters' (1969)[7]

* Fitt later became a member of the House of Lords.

Between 1962 and 1969, all these individuals and organisations, in their various ways, contributed to the most effective attack on Northern Ireland and its Protestant Unionist majority's failure to treat its Catholic minority with respect. And what many had in common was one Irishman – James Connolly – and the inspiration he provided.

As a teenager living in Kerry in the late 1960s it was RTE that brought the civil rights movement in Northern Ireland to life. In 1966 I watched the fiftieth celebrations of the Easter Rising, and on 5 October 1968 I saw live footage of policemen attacking marchers on the streets of Derry. This was a turning point in my political priorities. After this everything changed. The revolution was here, now, on our doorstep.

Chapter 10

AN ORGY OF
SELF-CONGRATULATION

1966 was a memorable year for many reasons, not least because it was the year England won the World Cup, and we could all see it on RTE television.

In Ireland it was also the anniversary of the Rising and the execution of its leaders by the English. But the fiftieth-anniversary celebrations were not only about the executions: there was the Famine, the Rebellion of 1798, Robert Emmet, Wolfe Tone, Kevin Barry, and 800 years of oppression.

Sean Lemass was seriously concerned about how to handle the celebrations. Like W. T. Cosgrave, though from a very different tradition, Lemass was a 1916 veteran, and his brother had been killed in very dubious circumstances by Free State forces acting extra-judicially. Lemass was another of those rather grey, uncharismatic politicians who almost never received the acclaim of the crowd. Yet it was politicians like Cosgrave and Lemass who gave substance to the new Irish state; they made it work, such as it did.

For many years Lemass had lived in the shadow of de Valera, and it was not until his retirement as Taoiseach that Lemass was able to effect the changes that would transform Ireland's economic base. The changes were dramatic, and the old Sinn Fein policy of protectionism and isolationism, which had kept the Republic a poverty-stricken, third-world country in all but geography, was finally binned.

Both Sinn Fein and the IRA were bitterly opposed to the new direction, as were backward elements in Lemass's own party. Both were afraid that the Gaelic Ireland which existed only in their imaginations would be drowned under a deluge of foreign capital and decadence.

The problem in 1966 for the modernisers was how to celebrate the Easter Rising and provide the framework for a new definition of patriotism that meant it was worthier and more noble to live and work for Ireland, boring as that sometimes might be, than fight and die gloriously and be remembered for ever among the pantheon of heroes. I can remember teachers telling us that it was now our duty to live for Ireland, and that it was no longer necessary to die because Ireland was free. There were other teachers, a minority, who held the view that Ireland was not yet free. What we were supposed to do about this was not spelled out, but it did not take

much imagination to understand that there was unfinished business and that the martyrs would not sleep easily
until the North was once again ours.

A major balancing act was required. In 1966 Ireland
was a very different place to the country it is now, but at
the time of writing and as we approach the hundredth
anniversary of the Rising the problem of the unfinished
business remains, both for Sinn Fein and for the dissidents
who believe that Gerry Adams and Martin McGuinness
have sold out. After the terror of the Long War of the
1970s and 1980s, when the morning news brought yet
another story about a horrible act of evil – though few in
polite society would admit it, too often a little whisper of
relief when it was not one of 'ours' – the difficulty is
perhaps more acute, athough there is always the sad but
invaluable knowledge of experience.

Yet even though Ireland was undergoing the changes
outlined in the previous chapter, it did not mean that this
mood of progress was sweeping through the Ireland I
knew. Development was slow, and certainly not all that
obvious in Kerry to someone who was not yet a
teenager.

What was it like for an eleven-year-old in the Ireland
of 1966? We were, of course, poor, as was most everyone
around. Our world was largely without washing machines,
vacuum cleaners (or even carpets), phones, supermarkets
or chain stores. I have a strong memory of women queuing
up on a Friday evening at the nearest public telephone
box, about a half mile away beside a grotto to the Blessed

Virgin, to take calls from husbands and boyfriends, sons and daughters who were working in Britain and who would confirm that they had been paid and had sent money home. No phone call might mean there would be little or no money that week.

To be honest, many of the hardships of adult life passed me by. We had enough to eat, mostly, clothes to wear, and not much expectation. Certainly we never went on holiday or anything like that. Football and reading were the two things that really interested me, as well as a little bit of fishing and wandering around the countryside, usually with dogs, looking for a rabbit or fox to amuse us. It was a mainly isolated and somewhat dreamlike existence, and looking back on it now I can see that it had much to recommend it.

When I see the tower blocks and the sordid streets where London's most marginalised people live, the grinding poverty of aspiration, the drugs, the prostitution, the loan sharks, the hopelessness, the Islamists scavenging for recruits among the desperate and inadequate as they offer the twin message of hate and glorious salvation as a get-out, I am glad, in spite of all that has happened, that I grew up in a world of fields and mostly innocent people, of grandparents and community.

The anniversary of the Rising completely dominated 1966 until about May. After that there was the World Cup. And, like everyone else around me, my family life was dominated by the Irish Catholic Church; I write 'Irish' quite deliberately and could just as easily have said the Irish Nationalist Catholic Church, in that it was remorselessly and singularly Irish, and we held a special place within the universal Catholic family.

The Gaelic Athletic Association was a secular religion and Gaelic football was its god in Kerry. Politics, fuelled by small-scale grubby corruption, was conservative, Nationalist and insular, and everything meshed together to create a grey uniform drabness that smothered ambition and initiative. Of course, people made their own fun but they made it against the tide.

It was a time when divorce, contraception and abortion were illegal. We were marched from primary school to confession on the first Friday of every month – but all this was normal to us, and because everything was Catholic we hardly thought about it. It was in the air we breathed. But I was too young in 1966 to understand the great social, material and cultural changes taking place within the country at large.

What I remember above all from that year is *Insurrection*, the RTE docu-drama depicting the Rising, and the constant return to the subject in school and the prayers. RTE devoted an enormous amount of time to its coverage, and I recall frequently wondering, 'Is there anything else on the telly?' There wasn't, of course, as we only had one channel.

For reasons I cannot clearly articulate it was Connolly, the man with the big moustache, who dominated *Insurrection* – perhaps it was because I heard the word 'socialist' and saw his connection with the Dublin lock-out and the strike of 1913. To me, socialism equalled good; I had obviously picked up something subliminal from my father, and more concretely from my peripheral reading around the subject. Maybe the word socialist was just controversial, a bad word and therefore attractive. What was more certain was that it was linked with the IRA and its paper *the United Irishman*, which was definitely radical and which I read furtively and excitedly.

I am far from alone among people of my age and older who recall *Insurrection* almost instantly when asked what they remember of the fiftieth anniversary. The novelist Colm Toibin wrote: 'The executions were drawn out, each moment dramatised – the grieving family, the grim prison, the lone leader in his cell, writing his last poem or letter. Sometimes the emotion in our house was unbearable, and when it came to James Connolly's turn to be executed my mother ran out of the room crying.'[1] Toibin was ten, and it was the first time he had seen his mother cry. According to the playwright, novelist and poet Dermot Bolger, 'For anyone who grew up in the 1960s, the Rising meant 1966 and not 1916.'[2] I could have written those words myself.

Born in 1958, Fintan O'Toole, columnist for the *Irish Times*, described 1966 as 'The year when 1916 needed to be divorced from all reality and turned into a movie ... that would run forever in the minds of a new generation in a new country and keep them loyal to the past. 1916 inured us to failure, befuddled us so that we don't know the difference between an inept tragedy of errors and a solid achievement.' He continued: 'It has given us a theatrical masochism, content with suffering so long as the gestures and symbols of defiance are right.'[3]

It is quite clear, as Roisin Higgins points out in *Transforming 1916*, that O'Toole's anger is directed at 1966 and was situated in the 1980s during the Long War. It is an anger shared by many of our generation at the failure to live up to what we perceived to be the promise of 1966. For many, the fiftieth celebrations appeared to glorify armed struggle and, in my opinion, played their part in the terrible events about to take place in Northern Ireland. And if it was like this for us in the South, what was it like for young Nationalists growing up in Northern Ireland in the mid-1960s in a place where the Republican movement played a much larger role in the commemorations? After all, it was in the North that the Unionists and the same British ruling class that executed our Irish martyrs still dominated.

And, even though we couldn't care less what they thought, how did the Unionists feel about all this? For David Trimble, '1916 had a particular legacy for the North, as the fiftieth anniversary of the rebellion started the destabilisation of Ulster.' He described it as an 'orgy of self-congratulation' that had a devastating impact on the position of moderate politics in Northern Ireland. Terence O'Neill, prime minister of Northern Ireland in 1966, described it in his own laconic fashion as 'not a very easy year'.[4]

It should also be remembered that it was only four

years since the last IRA campaign had ended, the Divis Street riots had occurred less than two years previously, and strong rumours of another IRA campaign were in the air. Something else was brewing too: there was talk of Republican and communist infiltration of trade unions and co-operation in the nascent civil rights movement itself.

1966 was also the fiftieth anniversary of the Battle of the Somme when over 2,000 members of the Ulster Volunteer Force had died in what was described as a year when Ulstermen lived up to their expectations of themselves. And in 1966 an organisation styling itself the UVF first made its appearance in Belfast and began attacking and killing those it believed to be enemies of the state.

I have since had many conversations with Loyalists who grew up during this period in Northern Ireland, and who were witness to this orgy of self-congratulation, as well as the rhetoric and the militarism from Republicans in Northern Ireland, where Dublin's writ did not run. They invariably saw the sentiments as repugnant and frightening, but also challenging as youths on the opposite side of the political divide were filled with excitement for the fight.

Whatever the intent, the celebrations of 1966 reopened old wounds. Forty years of windy Southern rhetoric about reclaiming our 'fourth green field', the slavish veneration of Pearse's ravings, the destructive wallowing in resentments real and imagined and always exaggerated, and the cynical nod and wink to the good old boys of the IRA – all this had created a sentimental, mawkish mess in which the ghoul of extreme Nationalism grew fat.

The celebrations got off to a real bang when a bomb blew up the iconic Nelson's Pillar in O'Connell Street, Dublin, in March 1966. This was not the official beginning, of course, but that distinction may well have been lost on Unionists who knew as little about the finer points of Republicanism or the Republic as we did about Unionism and Northern Ireland. The ensuing reaction to the destruction of the pillar also revealed the shadowy world of a Republican sub-state, a place where the IRA, and residual delinquent elements in Fianna Fail, existed in a sort of subterranean underworld.

A song written about the incident topped the Irish music charts for eight weeks. Titled 'Up Went Nelson', it was written and performed by four schoolteachers from Belfast. Writing about the O'Connell Street bomb now, I ask myself is it really any wonder that Unionists regarded this time as a moment of extreme self-congratulation, while many of us seemed to think that a large bomb in the centre of our capital city was a great joke, an act of defiance and morally acceptable. As late as 1969, when events in Northern Ireland had taken a very bloody twist indeed, the newly ordained Bishop of Kerry, Eamon Casey – later to become notorious for having fathered a child – decided to entertain the people at his ordination with a cheery rendition of 'The Merry Ploughboy', a song which celebrates the Rising and makes it sound like a grand day out.

The bomb exploded without warning at 1.30 a.m., scattering rubble along O'Connell Street. No one was injured but it could just as easily have caused carnage. Bombs are unpredictable and often result in bloodshed, as events in Northern Ireland would soon make us all too aware. But they were fun things in those days, all the more so when set to music. Most of our experience of bombs came from watching old footage of the Blitz, or listening to the folk group the Dubliners singing wittily about alarm clocks and gelignite and the IRA bombing campaign in England during 1939–40.

Official celebrations had started in February 1965 when the British government returned the remains of Sir Roger Casement, who was then buried in Glasnevin cemetery after a state funeral on 1 March. Casement had been arrested just before the Rising, after being dropped off from a German submarine. At the same time, loaded with German weapons, the Norwegian-registered ship, the *Aud*, was intercepted by the British and eventually scuttled by its commander in Cork harbour. The weapons and support had been supplied by our 'gallant allies in Europe' – but who were these allies? As well as the Germans, another component of the alliance was the Ottoman Empire, which in 1915 carried out the genocide of about one million Armenians. It is, of course, quite possible that neither Casement nor the other Irish leaders knew anything of the Armenian genocide, but

Irish Republicans have a long tradition, stretching to the present day, of not being too particular about potential allies as long as they share England as a common enemy.

In fact, the Irish state has always had a problem about how to celebrate 1916. When the Free State government had its first official ceremony in 1924, only the relatives of one executed leader, Michael Mallon, showed up. The others had taken the anti-Treaty side and believed the government had sold out the Republic. There was also some difficulty about nominating an Independence Day since this would only draw attention to the failure to achieve independence for the entire island, as well as to the subsequent Civil War. In the end, an official Independence Day was impossible, so Cumann na nGhael and later Fine Gael tried to mark independence with commemorations for Michael Collins and Arthur Griffith, but without anything resembling national support.

The only people who for fifty years had consistently celebrated 1916, both as a life source and a stick to beat the Free State Establishment with, was the Republican movement, which meant essentially the mostly illegal IRA.

In parts of the country, like it or lump it, the IRA had a very strong claim on the 'brand'. Therefore, in some areas, as in Tralee, the unofficial celebrations were often larger and more numerous than the sporadic and somewhat half-hearted official ones. Of course, when it wanted to, the Irish government could provide far bigger resources than the Republican movement, but it remained disputed and troubled territory.

A good example of where the unofficial commemorations attracted more support than the government-sponsored ones was in County Leitrim, the birthplace of Sean McDermott, one of the executed 1916 leaders. Aside from Dublin, Leitrim was one of the twelve official locations designated by the government, but a problem arose almost immediately when the sisters and niece of McDermott objected to the celebrations and released a statement saying: 'We are true to the 32-county Republic for which all these Leitrim men, including Sean, died, and we object to commemoration ceremonies organised by those who have accepted less.'[5]

The result was two ceremonies in Kiltyclogher on Easter Sunday. The *Sligo Champion* newspaper reported that the official military parade was held in the presence of only a couple of hundred onlookers, while the afternoon ceremony, organised by the National Graves Association (a Republican organisation which looks after the monuments and memorials to martyrs), was attended by a large crowd.

The year or so leading up to the Rising commemoration was marked by a number of small-scale violent incidents primarily in the south-eastern corner of Ireland, in which Richard Behal, then a young, some would say charismatic and certainly erratic Republican activist, began to make a name for himself. Shots were also fired at a British naval vessel, a telephone exchange in County Kilkenny was blown up, roads were blocked and rioting broke out following court appearances. Behal was sentenced to nine months imprisonment and subsequently escaped from Limerick Prison.

The Irish police had begun a clampdown on the sale of Easter lily paper badges which the Republican movement sold every Easter to raise funds. I remember scuffles over Easter lilies between Republicans and the police at the church gate in Tralee, and it was obvious whose side most of the onlookers were on. It was exciting but harmless, and it was also clear that the hearts of most of the police present were not really in it. The violent activity of Behal and his small group infuriated IRA leaders like Goulding and Garland; it was exactly the kind of stuff they were trying to get away from. For me, it just confirmed the romantic Robin Hood image of the IRA.

In Northern Ireland everything was different, darker and more serious, for here was disputed ownership of territory. This is where the killing was done.

In 1966 the police in Northern Ireland were on high alert. Rumours flourished as tensions grew amid speculation as to the IRA's intentions and capabilities. Events like the blowing up of Nelson's Pillar in Dublin, although the work of individual IRA men and not sanctioned by the leadership, did nothing to calm Unionists, many of whom were inclined to think that all Republican activity was masterminded from Dublin, or even Rome.

In the North any commemoration of the 1916 Rising was always going to be a challenge to the very existence of the Province. No matter how peaceful the protests, they were bound to provoke tension – and helped by the rise of Ian Paisley, they certainly did. And even though intelligence reports from the Royal Ulster Constabulary that year suggested that Loyalists were a bigger security threat than the IRA, this cannot possibly have been how most Unionists saw it. Easter Sunday parades by Republicans, confined mainly to Nationalist areas, had passed off relatively peacefully in the past, but the plans for the fiftieth anniversary were of a different magnitude.

There was also the fact that for most Unionists any celebration of the Easter Rising was a slap in the face for their dead at the Somme. Then, as now, in Northern Ireland one community's celebration provoked resentment and hostility in the other. It should also be said that Republicans had every intention of using the celebrations to provoke the state, because that is what they did. In so doing, they also hoped to gain recruits and raise the profile of their cause.

The years between 1964 and 1966 had seen a rise in sectarian tension, particularly in Belfast. According to writer Bob Purdie, 'In 1966 communalist incidents took on a more serious character than usual. There was a clustering of cases of arson, desecration, violence and intimidation. It was the year of the Cromac Street riot,* of the blowing

---

* Ian Paisley tried to lead a march through the Nationalist markets area.

up of Nelson's Pillar in Dublin, and of the emergence of the UVF.' In September, Lord Chief Justice Lord MacDermott told the grand jury at the opening of the Belfast City Commission that 'It had been a period of some tumult ... some rioting and violence ... You may well reach the conclusion that the gunman has come amongst us again.'[6]

The most sinister development in 1966 was the emergence of the UVF from the Loyalist community among the back streets of Belfast. Later, it claimed to have been formed both in response to the fiftieth-anniversary celebrations and the perceived threat of renewed IRA violence.

The new UVF was a different sort of Loyalist organisation. Small, secretive and clustered in the main around a group of individuals in the Shankill Road area of Belfast, it set out to kill people it perceived to be enemies of the state. And, in the absence of a Republican, it was often said that any Catholic would do. There have always been rumours that the UVF was masterminded by key players within the Unionist community, but there is precious little hard evidence of this. I have met Loyalists who firmly believe that Rome or John Hume or some powerful Catholic organisation pulled the strings of the IRA. I have also met Nationalists who believe that the UVF was the military wing of the Unionist Establishment, who were in turn directed by formidable right-wing elements in Great Britain. Displacement is a wonderful instrument.

Paisley in particular was often linked to the shadowy,

violent fringe of the Loyalists, though he was no friend
to the Unionist Establishment. But, while no direct
involvement was ever proven, there can be no doubt that
he was guilty of fanning the flames of sectarian hatred.
It is my firm opinion that today in any secular society
he would be described as a religious 'hate preacher' and
almost certainly prosecuted.

The fact remained that throughout 1966 the UVF
murdered or attempted to murder a number of Roman
Catholics in Northern Ireland. It was immediately
declared an illegal organisation, and the police quickly
rounded up many of those directly responsible for the
murders.

Down in Kerry, and heading into my teenage years,
all this was certainly in the news, but my youthful interest
in politics was much more directed at social and cultural
conditions south of the border. I can more clearly
remember an RTE programme called *Seven Days*
exposing the activities of moneylenders in Ireland and
the controversy this generated than I can those of the
UVF in what was then faraway Belfast.

Thus it was that the first forty years or so of the Irish
state had seen Pearse emerge and subsequently remain
unrivalled as the embodiment of all that was good about
the Irish soul. But in 1966 Connolly, in so many ways
Pearse's direct opposite, rose as a figure of equal importance. Pearse, while a great Irishman, represented the
old Ireland. I wasn't interested in the restoration of the
Irish language, or the Catholic Church with all its

arrogance, or the glorification of the peasant idyll. I could see the reality of all this every day, and even as a boy I could also see the hypocrisy that seeped through every aspect of it.

It was Connolly and the startling, defiant realism of his words that set my brain on fire. I also have to say that my reading about the sheer perseverance of the IRA from the Civil War onwards, through the dog days of the 1940s and 1950s – these guys who never gave up, who kept the flame alive – added to this fire. In my view, Charlie Kerins did not murder a policeman, but he himself was murdered by Free State traitors who borrowed a British hangman for the job. My version of events was heavily influenced by my father. This was the world of the sect, of the malcontent and the marginalised.

Connolly's words, or at least his better-known quotes and phrases, also impacted on me. 'Ireland without her people is nothing to me' might seem pretty obvious, but when you remember that hundreds of thousands of Irish men and women were forced to emigrate to 'pagan' England to find work, it makes a lot more sense. Or that Pearse's Ireland subjected many of its own children to an experiment in Catholic Nationalist Gothic horror, the violence and ugliness of which is only now being fully revealed, as is the sexual abuse of children and its cover-up by the Church and government institutions, and not forgetting the casually administered brutality in industrial-school borstals located often in the most remote places, the scandal of the Magdalene laundries, and the grotesque subordination of women, who truly were second-class citizens and barely citizens at all in some cases. I wrote earlier that I was glad to grow up in a largely innocent world. The truth is that it was a world of secrecy and obedience in which criticism and enquiry were forbidden options.

To my young mind, Connolly was different, or perhaps it is truer to say that the ideology he espoused was different. When I first read the words of Sean Lemass, who said in 1966, 'I have no doubt that if James Connolly was alive today he would be with the Fianna Fail party in what we are trying to do,' I thought it was a barefaced lie – and it was. But I now think it possible that Lemass was perhaps unconsciously hitting at something else. Connolly was modern, his voice and politics resonated with a younger, less conservative Ireland, and Lemass was annexing anything he thought suited his own, more liberal agenda.

And there was little doubt that as Ireland moved into the 1960s the public mood yearned for reality and did not want the Ireland of myths and fairies. Connolly was the hard man, the realist rooted in real life, in grinding poverty, in work and trade unions, but still a martyr prepared to die for his cause. That he was a Marxist and an internationalist was also significant, and he was heralded as a champion of workers' rights, the emancipation of women, a truly secular society and, of course, a united Ireland.

Students at Queen's University in Belfast were also

adopting the language of socialism and world revolution, and Connolly and Guevara were their icons. Foremost among them were Bernadette Devlin and Michael Farrell, who would play a crucial part in pushing the civil rights movement into a direct and violent confrontation with the Unionist state. In Derry, Eamonn McCann, a young Trotskyite, was railing against the more cautious elements, such as older communists like Greaves and Sinclair, who despaired of these youthful and ignorant 'chancers', as she described them. Sinclair, Greaves and the more moderate Nationalist leaders knew from experience that aggressive demands for civil rights and street disorder would provoke a fierce response from the Northern Ireland state as well as the Loyalist working class, who would see it as an attack on them.

I was sold on Connolly lock, stock and barrel, from the word go. When the civil rights movement exploded onto our television screens on 5 October 1968 I was fourteen. As an avowed and very presumptuous Connollyite, I had read some of his easier works and knew several quotes off by heart. My attempt to read Marx's *Das Kapital* came to an abrupt end when I saw that it contained *x*s and *y*s and unfamiliar symbols, far too like algebra, and I found it utterly incomprehensible and tedious. What I wanted was rhetoric and excitement. Connolly, the events in Northern Ireland, my general stroppiness and my one-man war against the 'establishment' – mostly my parents and school – provided that.

And so it was that I read more Connolly, more IRA

history, more Guevara, got more bored with school, and became an even more obnoxious, arrogant and troubled teenager as the strife in Northern Ireland began to fill our newspapers and television screens. The images we saw nightly were dominated by violence, by Ian Paisley, bigoted and brutish, and by Bernadette Devlin, young, female, articulate and fiery. We all knew which side we were on.

Then, in 1969, the North finally exploded, first in Derry, then in Belfast. My memory is of endless television-watching of Catholic houses burning, of refugees streaming across the border to safety, of the Irish Army and Reserves being mobilised. And, of course, British troops were once again on Irish streets, but this time to protect Nationalists from Loyalist attacks, sometimes assisted by the RUC and B-Specials. I remember a well-attended public meeting in Tralee in which one speaker reminded the crowd that there was another army in Ireland, and his remark being greeted with cheers. It seemed obvious to me that the Nationalists in Northern Ireland had been defeated, at least for now, so where was this other army? Where was the IRA?

It soon became clear that the Republican movement was deeply split over the events in Northern Ireland. I had little understanding of the underlying reasons for this, but paramount to me was its complete failure to defend the Nationalists fighting on the streets in Belfast and Derry, even though there is now plenty of evidence to show that the IRA was much more active, if largely ineffective, than the popular version has it.

Brought up on a diet of a glorious fighting force, of a mythical secret army ready to fight and die for Ireland, this was a great disappointment. But a secret army existing as any kind of fighting force really was a myth. It only existed in the minds of a few fanatics, the foolish younger Nationalists in Northern Ireland who thought they could depend on it, and the truly deluded – of whom I was one.

Chapter 11

THE GREEN

By the late-1960s I only attended school when there was no way out of it. Sometimes I turned up and left when I felt like it, other times I just didn't bother going in. The only subjects that held the slightest interest for me were history and English. The others, with the possible exception of geography, seemed alien to me. I couldn't stand the whole Gaelic, religious, Christian Brothers-dominated ethos of The Green, as the secondary school I went to was known, because it stood on the fringes of the town park that had been donated to the town by the Anglo-Irish Denny family.

Sometime around my third year in secondary school I left and went to the local technical school, which had long been looked down on. The move didn't make much difference to my attendance or interest, except that economics and economic history appealed to me. Even so, I didn't want to be there. I wanted to be in Northern Ireland where the action was. Reading Connolly, Guevara, Lenin and Castro was all fine, but they advocated action – and there wasn't much of that on a rainy day in Tralee in early 1970. I was bored; arrogant and bored.

Meanwhile events on both sides of the border were moving very quickly. The Irish general election in July 1969 had returned Fianna Fail to power, now led by the mild-looking Cork man Jack Lynch. Lemass had resigned as Taoiseach in November 1966, believing that it was time to hand over to a new generation. As events transpired there is a case to be made that he was sorely missed during what became not only an internal crisis for Fianna Fail but a crisis for Ireland.

The big loser in the Irish general election of June 1969 was the Irish Labour Party. It was the party of James Connolly, which after an absence of forty years had redis-covered the word socialism. Fired up with new recruits such as Conor Cruise O'Brien and David Thornley it set out, in the words of its leader, Brendan Corish, to make the 1970s socialist. Unfortunately for them Fianna Fail knew exactly what to do in such circumstances. Unleashing the Red Scare weapon, they claimed that the Irish Labour Party had been infiltrated by commies, of whom Connor Cruise O'Brien was the scariest of all.

O'Brien was one of the strangest of beasts in Irish politics, an intellectual and a socialist, who must there-fore be a communist. O'Brien describes how, shortly after this time, his wife listened to a priest deliver a sermon in Dingle, County Kerry. 'Socialism,' the priest said, 'is worse than Communism. Socialism is a heresy of Communism. Socialists are a Protestant variety of Communists.'[1]

Lynch toured the country and the convents and was pictured on television nodding wisely with nuns. O'Brien got himself elected in Dublin, where such tactics did not quite carry the same weight. Instead of gaining seats, Labour lost some of the ones it already held, mostly because it ran a woeful campaign characterised by intellectual arrogance and talking down to ordinary people. In Kerry, Dan Spring, far removed from intellectual and socialist nonsense, ran his home-grown campaign and was elected as usual.

The 1969 election was the first one I have a conscious memory of, and to me it was dominated by the aforementioned Red Scare. I also remember arguments among older people about whether O'Brien was a good Irishman. Their position was that because he was a divorcee he could not be a good Catholic or a good Irishman. They also felt he had ideas above his station.

My only problem with O'Brien was that I hoped he really was a revolutionary Marxist. My sympathies were also tied up with the leftward drift of the IRA and Sinn Fein, which I fully supported and I could not understand why the people around me failed to see how right they were, although I wasn't surprised because most of the older people I knew were boring, stupid, and sheep-like.

*　　*　　*

In December 1969 the Republican movement finally split. It was inevitable that the political and socialist strategy the leadership had adopted would lead many of the old guard to leave in disgust or just drift away. This had been happening for some time. Those that remained loyal to the existing leadership saw themselves as totally within the Connolly tradition. This was a world view they broadly shared with many of the new standard bearers of the Left in the Irish Labour Party.

The split was equally about the old, thorny and somewhat theological issue of abstentionism. Sinn Fein was still refusing to take seats if elected in the Dail, and refusing to recognise the legitimacy of any government sitting in Dublin. They also held that the IRA's authority as the real government derived from the last all-Ireland election in 1918. For some of the older, traditional members this was an article of faith that was above discussion. Taking seats in Dublin or Belfast meant accepting a settlement that did not recognise a true Republic. Going down this road meant membership of yet another constitutional party, being house-trained and corrupted by the venality of power and, to paraphrase Orwell, becoming a revolutionary who was a social climber without a gun. And I agreed with them. In the context of the reality of life in Ireland at the time it was an entirely delusional opinion.

But it was about much more than this. The people who broke away to form the Provisional IRA had long been unhappy with what they believed was a Marxist takeover of their movement. They had seen the influence of Johnston, and by implication Greaves, and they believed that the IRA had become so concerned with politics that it had neglected its primary duty, which was to protect Nationalists in Northern Ireland. There is, however, recent evidential research which shows that the IRA was more active in Belfast in August 1969 than had been commonly supposed.

My understanding of all this was that the Marxists and socialist Republicans gathered around Goulding and his close associates had cocked it all up by deciding to take seats in the Irish parliament, if elected. What I wanted was a revolutionary force that would destroy the bourgeois democracy, defeat the British in the North and overthrow their capitalist lackeys in the South. Contesting elections and going into parliament was not revolutionary. It was also boring. Many of my friends today would describe this young man as a 'delinquent Trot', and they would be right. It would all have been perfectly harmless nonsense – except for one thing: the North, and the events taking place there, was a bloody reality. The people who had formed the Provisional IRA were clear about one thing; they would fight the British, no ifs, no buts, just as Connolly had.

I was also hugely influenced by the example of the radical students of the People's Democracy. Based at Queen's University in Belfast, they ignored the voices of reason who wanted a truce with Terence O'Neill to allow him time to introduce promised reforms in Northern

Ireland. They were publicly represented by Bernadette Devlin, Michael Farrell and associates such as the Derry Trotskyite Eamonn McCann, and when they went ahead with their 'long march' from Belfast to Derry in January 1969 they pushed aside the moderate leadership of the civil rights movement, the cautious communists like Greaves, Sinclair and Johnston, as well as the Republican leadership close to Goulding and the older Nationalist stalwarts.

Their march took them through some fiercely Loyalist areas and eventually they were ambushed at Burntollet by enraged Loyalists, aided by off-duty paramilitary police. The television images of the attack were brutal and highly effective from the marchers' viewpoint. By taking action, the students and their supporters had played a huge role in finishing off any notion that all Northern Ireland needed was a little tinkering at the edges.

I was ecstatic. This was what it was all about – direct action, no more pussyfooting with the system that needed to be destroyed north and south of the border. Sean MacStiofain, the first chief of staff of the Provisional IRA and then one of the chief opponents of Goulding and his supporters, praised the bravery of the students who had finally seen off the belief that Northern Ireland could be re-formed.

I had yet to set foot in Northern Ireland, had never met a Northern Unionist, but I was seized by an absolute certainty that this was a fight I wanted to be part of. Strengthened by the iconic figure of Connolly, the stories, songs and myths of Ireland's centuries-old fight for freedom and the humiliations it had suffered, my young life suddenly had a purpose.

The British were the enemy, as was the Irish Free State Establishment, who were simply lackeys of British imperialism. Unionists, if I thought about them at all, were deceived both by the British and the Orangemen, and once they realised this and came to agree with us, which they surely would, all would be well. I can and do laugh at this now, but my fantasies were not that different from many others who lived as I did in the twisted world of Nationalist socialist militancy. It was an Irish version of fascism – but it was fascism nonetheless.

It was around February of 1970 when I first applied to join the Provisional IRA, only to be told that I would have to join Sinn Fein first, which I did. The first meeting I attended took place in Connolly Hall – where else? – which was the Tralee branch office of the ITGWU. The person who chaired the meeting was named Kevin Barry, a local businessman who had once been a Fianna Fail councillor and was named after the eighteen-year-old IRA martyr executed during the War of Independence.

I can still remember vividly how he described the difference between the Provisional IRA and the group that became known as the Official IRA. It was a Sinn Fein meeting but he seemed to conflate the two, at times saying IRA and at others Sinn Fein, though it barely mattered. The Provisionals (of whom I was now one) were 'green', the others were 'red'; the Provisionals were Nationalist, anti-communist and Catholic; the Officials were communists and anti-Nationalist.

I remember thinking, 'I hope I've made the right call here,' and also deducing as Kevin Barry spoke that the Officials wanted to go into parliament in Dublin and hadn't shown much appetite for defending the Nationalists in Northern Ireland. I also remember thinking that I would be okay because Connolly had linked up with Pearse and other people like him, and attempted to use them. I saw the Provisionals as a broad popular front that would achieve freedom, and then socialism would sweep away the old order, and proclaim the Worker's Republic. At fifteen I was obviously a lot smarter than anyone else in that room.

I spent most of 1970 selling Sinn Fein's newspapers, collecting money for Northern Aid (as we called it) and generally being involved in Sinn Fein's local organisation. I was still at school but taking little or no interest in it. Apart from that, I was going to dances, youth clubs, still playing some football, hanging out in cafés, listening to music, and reading, always reading. I was also dreaming of getting away, because the drab reality of life in small-town rural Ireland was not changing as much as I wanted it to.

Then sometime in the late summer, a few months shy of my sixteenth birthday, I finally got to join the IRA, an event that changed my life for ever, and will impact on it until the day I die. It also affected other people's lives in a brutal manner, and would go on to affect the lives of those close to me in ways I could not possibly have foreseen.

Ireland, in the meantime, was being convulsed by what came to be known as the Arms Crisis. In May 1970 the Taoiseach, Jack Lynch, announced the dismissal of two senior government ministers, Charles Haughey and Neil Blaney, because of suspicions that they were involved in an illegal plot to import weapons into Ireland for the defence of Northern Nationalists, who were almost certainly the Provisional IRA or groups under their influence.

How much Lynch and other members of the government knew about this is unclear, though the fact remained that he only took action when made aware by Liam Cosgrave, the leader of the main opposition party, Fine Gael, who publicly said it was 'a situation of such gravity for the nation that it is without parallel in this country since the foundation of the state'.

It has since been stated that the Arms Crisis went to the core of what Irish democracy was all about, but to me it was proof of the state's uselessness and cowardice in defending Northern Nationalists. Why was it wrong to train and arm Nationalists to defend themselves against Loyalists and the British Army? Why shouldn't the IRA take weapons wherever they could get them, even if it was from the most unpleasant elements in Fianna Fail? It all proved to me that Southern politics and politicians were corrupt and venal. They talked a good talk, but when it came to it their Nationalist brothers in the North just didn't matter. Our approach – my approach – was straightforward: we would do whatever we could to fight back.

My first IRA meeting took place on a fairly large, well-managed farm not too far from Tralee. I went through no induction ceremony of any kind, which was not that unusual in those days. I was collected, along with a couple of others I already knew, by Kevin Barry and we drove to the farm. We went into an elevated grain shed and a mound of grain was shovelled away to reveal a collection of guns and ammunition. I knew most of the people there by sight, and our job was to clean the weapons and sort out the ammunition according to which gun it belonged to. The guns were old but perfectly serviceable Lee-Enfield .303 rifles, Sten guns, Thompson sub-machine guns and a collection of pistols and revolvers.* The people who minded them, like most of the other Republicans in the area, had broken with the IRA a couple of years previously because of the policies the leadership was pursuing, and had held on to these weapons, which were now going to be sent to the Provisional IRA in Northern Ireland.

I was becoming increasingly immersed in the world of

---

* Many years later, in Westminster, David Trimble quoted from my account of this meeting in my book *The Informer* to show why decommissioning of weapons is so necessary. I am still passionately convinced he was right.

the IRA, and it was a secret world of lies and evasion and conspiracy. While going to school or hanging around with my pals, I felt estranged, different. I didn't tell my friends or my family I was in the IRA, though they knew I'd joined Sinn Fein. My father knew I was in the IRA but never really mentioned it. You just didn't. I belonged to something that demanded loyalty: if you were prepared to die for Ireland, you should certainly be prepared to lie for Ireland.

It was also a fiercely elitist world; I belonged to a movement that was selective and powerful, and had the authority of life or death over its enemies and its members. It was exciting, seductive and it certainly beat listening to some teacher droning on about civics. It was then, and is now, a key tenet of indoctrination to create a family within a family, a home within a home, a state within a state, where the everyday rules do not apply. Indoctrination also teaches that the outside world constantly encroaches on the life of the radical who resides in the liberal state. Opportunity, work, love, music, material things, all the paraphernalia of Western life – it makes you soft. Being a true believer demands total commitment to a cause that is absolute and perfect, and which you are willing to go to jail for, to kill or be killed for.

Reading Connolly now I am often struck by how he is never happy in the present, this very instant. He is always reaching for some kind of perfection. Nothing and no one is ever good enough. I feel I want to scream at him: eat a bloody ice cream, go for a walk in the park, lighten up. It is all about struggle, sacrifice, anger, conflict, and talk of conflict. There is no sense that he ever enjoyed life. There is no room for compassion for other human beings; they are merely parts of his vision of how the world should be. The rich are despised because they are rich, the poor because they are too stupid or cowardly to fight. Connolly knows precisely what is wrong with the world and he is determined to make it bow to his will. There never was or ever could be any room for self-doubt.

And looking back now on how I felt when I joined the Provisional IRA, there was no doubt in my mind either: I was doing something I believed in. I had joined a cause that I was prepared to fight for and, if necessary, die for.

Chapter 12

ONE OF THE CHOSEN FEW

As violence came to dominate life in Northern Ireland my involvement with the Provisional IRA increased. My new life left little room for anything else. After receiving rudimentary training in the use of guns and explosives I was tasked with training recruits. At first they were local, then as 1970 went on recruits were sent from Northern Ireland on a regular basis as the organisation became more structured and focused.

I say recruits but because of the quick growth of the Provisional IRA and the chaotic nature of the violence in Belfast many of the men who joined me had already experienced serious rioting, gun battles and bombings. But in other cases Provisional IRA members with no knowledge whatsoever of weapons had guns pressed into their hands and were told to start shooting.

The recruitment process was pretty shambolic, and

any notion that they were carefully picking and vetting members who then went through a system of education, political and military, is a fantasy. In essence, the Provisionals were a largely apolitical movement, driven primarily by a desire to protect Catholics, particularly in Belfast, and then to retaliate, drawing in the British Army before moving to an offensive war against the state and the army.

At least that was the plan, but these were chaotic times and events in the early 1970s quickly assumed a life of their own. What the Provisionals had was a tradition that supplied a story of continuity concerning the struggle against the British, and a supply of very angry people hell-bent on revenge. We also benefited from the fact that any honeymoon period the British Army enjoyed with the Nationalists was almost certain to be short-lived. Even though the army had been sent in to protect Catholics, the reality was that it was an arm of the British state that wanted to restore order to Northern Ireland.

Throughout 1970 and 1971, the Provisional IRA made gigantic strides recruiting support among the Catholic population. Irish-American help, in the form of money and guns, was also invaluable when it came to producing a cohesive armed group capable of sustaining a high-intensity campaign of violence. And in the South of Ireland some members of Fianna Fail, in particular, were willing to provide financial support as long as the Provisionals confined their activities to the North.

Fighting the British in Northern Ireland was okay,

these individuals reasoned, but there was to be none of that Marxist nonsense in the South, and certainly no IRA attempts to undermine or attack a Dublin government. Many politicians and security advisers in the South identified the Official IRA as a far greater political threat because their leadership was seen as politically intelligent and therefore far more dangerous to the Southern conservative Catholic Nationalist Establishment. Many in the Official IRA were Connollyites, which meant they took their Socialist politics seriously. Neither were they prepared to give up their political agitation in the South in return for being allowed to operate in Northern Ireland. It was not unusual to meet members and supporters of Fianna Fail, and indeed of other political parties, who would say, 'We're all IRA,' when what they really meant was: 'We support Nationalists in the North in their fight, but don't challenge us down here.'

Many senior members of the Official IRA and Sinn Fein welcomed the split between their two organisations. They were glad to be rid of what they saw as right-wing traditional Catholic gunmen who made up the Provisionals, and many senior Provisionals were happy to be rid of the so-called communists who wanted to enter the Irish parliament. Of course, the Officials soon found themselves immediately competing against the Provisionals, particularly in Belfast, who offered far simpler solutions and did not care what politics a young man had as long as he knew that the Brits and the Unionists were the enemy, and was able to fire a gun or plant a bomb.

There is no doubt in my mind that most of the leadership of the Official IRA sought to defuse the situation by bringing real politics to bear within the civil rights movement, the trade unions and their own supporters. But this was always going to be an uphill struggle against the backdrop of daily sectarian violence and the Provisional IRA's urgency to engage militarily with the British.

By the spring of 1971 I was regularly attending training camps where there was little, if any, talk of politics. We had the occasional lecture on the history of Ireland as written by the Provisional IRA, which placed great emphasis on the suffering and self-sacrifice of Republicans over the centuries. Because the camps were in Kerry there was a particular focus on the wickedness of the Irish Free State, and it was emphasised that true Republicans would never recognise or participate in either of the partitionist parliaments in Dublin and Belfast, which were illegal assemblies; those who participated in them, including the leadership of the Official IRA, were traitors and would be dealt with when the time was right.

It was an extraordinary world. The only thing that was real was the ongoing certainty of what was happening in Northern Ireland, though how we interpreted this was an altogether different matter. We believed that the British held Northern Ireland by force, against the wishes of the Irish people. And we believed that the IRA had a moral duty and a historical imperative to drive them out. Protestants had been duped by the British into believing that they were not Irish – but they were, and would come to their senses once the British had gone. In the meantime we would have to fight and kill them because they were killing Catholics. We also believed that although the Southern Irish leaders were traitors, many of their supporters were sound on the North and would rally to us once the British had left. We were the pure, the chosen few, following in a long tradition of those who had never surrendered. Or, as the words of 'Take it down from the Mast', an anti-Treaty IRA song written in 1923 by James Ryan has it, we were: 'The men who intend to do killing ... Until England's tyranny cease.'

We were also of the opinion that the Irish people as a whole had never truly deserved freedom. Most of them were slave-like, and happy to leave it to people like us to do the killing and dying for them. Always we had endured, suffered, gone to jail, died on hunger strike or by the enemy's hand. After the Republic of All Ireland was declared, the country would be governed under an ancient form of communitarianism where everyone would be equal and Gaelic.

Did we really believe all this? We did, more or less. But first we had to drive the Brits out and protect the Catholics from the Protestants. This was a land governed by the moral imperative of 1916. For as Patrick Pearse had quoted: 'That in every generation / Must Ireland's blood be shed' (W.B. Yeats, 'Three Songs to the One Burden', 1938.)

*   *   *

The introduction of internment in August 1971, which affected people from the Nationalist community only, was characterised by poor police intelligence, ineptitude and in many instances a degree of undue harshness or overzealousness by soldiers ill-equipped for such a task. Belfast erupted in violence and both the Official and Provisional IRA engaged in prolonged gun battles with the British Army and with Loyalists.

In many parts of the South young men enquired about joining the IRA, and sales of papers and funding increased dramatically. As so often happened in Southern Ireland, however, this rarely translated into anything long-lasting or substantial. Emotions would rise, but they would just as quickly subside, leaving us to mutter bitterly that the Irish people just weren't up to it. They were soft and more than ready to let us do their dirty work for them. This especially applied to the politicians.

After the intense violence following internment had abated there was a renewed flood of recruits to the training camps in Kerry. This kept me busy but also left me deeply frustrated because I wanted to be sent to Northern Ireland. Technically I was still at school and somehow I managed to avoid being expelled. I still found time to read, devouring everything I could get my hands on about every national liberation campaign and movement. I also read Connolly and Fintan Lalor, Wolfe Tone and Liam Mellows. They all had one thing in common: they could be described as coming from the left of Irish Republicanism.

In April 1972 I finished up in jail after explosives I had been working on for a training camp blew up in a shed in the backyard of our home. So there I was, seventeen years old and on remand in Limerick Prison, charged with possession of explosives, a gun and ammunition. I was the youngest prisoner there, certainly the only inmate under twenty-one. Again, I remember reading quite a lot during that time. For reasons I can't fully record now, my old headmaster was keen for me to sit my Leaving Certificate, which I did. In June of that year I appeared before the special criminal court in Dublin. As instructed, I refused to recognise the authority of the court, and was sentenced to six months' imprisonment. I served out the rest of the sentence in Dublin's Mountjoy Prison. It was during this time that my grandmother died. I was refused permission to attend her funeral.

Before I was arrested in 1972, Bloody Sunday happened on 30 January in Derry and was one of the defining incidents of what became known as the Troubles. I remember watching television that evening with older and more senior Republicans who were convinced that the events of Bloody Sunday had been planned at the highest levels of the British government and sanctioned by the prime minister.

I never believed this conspiracy. Yes, the soldiers were psyched up, and there surely were anti-Irish, racist attitudes among some of the soldiers and officers serving in Northern Ireland. But it just did not seem credible to me that Perfidious Albion, the sophisticated, cynical, ruthless political operators that designed and ran the British Empire, would think it was clever to shoot down unarmed civilians in part of the United Kingdom and in full view of television cameras. The army had behaved appallingly and the politicians responsible were guilty of complacency and arrogance, but they did not order soldiers to murder innocent civilians.

Today a lot of people might agree with me, though perhaps not all. But it was not like that in January 1972 in any place where Irish Nationalists gathered, and in the weeks that followed the Provisional IRA ramped up its campaign. When caught up in the noise of the next bang, the next dead soldier, the next dead policeman, it is easy to believe you are winning. It was a period that culminated on 21 July with Bloody Friday, when over twenty Provisional IRA bombs exploded in Belfast killing nine people and injuring many more. Warnings were given but proved hopelessly inadequate.

Once again I watched the news coverage, which included graphic descriptions of body parts being placed in plastic bags. I remember my mother saying to me when atrocities like this occurred, 'No good will come of this' and 'Before it's all over no one will know or care who started it.' But at the time I just couldn't bring myself to listen to her.

Bloody Friday was followed by Operation Motorman, when the British Army moved to take control of no-go areas in Belfast and Derry. It would, in retrospect, mark the end of the high point of the Provisional IRA's military campaign. Never again would it enjoy such unambiguous control of territory as it had before.

By March 1972 a key demand of the Provisional IRA – that the Stormont parliament be prorogued and direct rule from Westminster implemented – was met. It was said to be a temporary measure, but what it meant from the IRA's perspective was that it was now engaged directly in a war with the British government. It was exactly how the IRA loved to portray the conflict. This helped to make it 'clean': it was us, the Irish, against the occupying Brits.

Although the Provisional IRA may have been a mostly apolitical movement, it was not entirely devoid of politics. Some people in its leadership had been involved in Sinn Fein over the years, but their politics were often crude and could be summed up as 'Brits out'. Theirs was fundamentally a deep loathing of constitutional politics, of politics that required debate and compromise, and where the influence was measured in votes received, not in violence meted out to their opponents.

On the ground the Provisionals were throwing everything they had at Northern Ireland, and Loyalists were hitting back, mainly by murdering Catholics and Republicans, the ethnic rage that was hot-wired into the conflict becoming worse as atrocity fuelled bloody revenge. It did not matter how much the Provisional leadership might try to pretend that this was a clear-cut war of liberation to end British occupation; the reality that was a million Protestants, who had lived in Northern Ireland for near 400 years, just kept intruding.

But the IRA thought it had the upper hand, and when a delegation met with representatives of the British government in London in July, we really did believe we were on the high road to achieving our dream of driving the British out and securing national freedom.

It truly was the most extraordinary situation. The British government, in the persons of home secretary Willie Whitelaw, junior Northern Ireland minister Paul Channon and senior MI6 officer John Steele, met with the IRA leadership at Channon's house in Cheyne Walk, Chelsea. There was no pretence that they were meeting with Sinn Fein; the IRA men had no verifiable democratic mandate, and they had never contested an election. It is hard to know who on the British side supported this initiative or what they expected to gain from it.

Gerry Adams, released from internment as a precondition, Martin McGuinness, Dave O'Connell, Seamus Twomey and Sean MacStiofain (the last three now dead), made up the IRA delegation, complete with solicitor Myles Shevlin. Their demand was simple: the British government should commit to withdrawing from Northern Ireland by 1975.

The talks were not just ill-conceived on the British side, they were profoundly foolish, the motive being along the lines of, 'It's about time we had a look at these chaps.'

There was little consultation within the British Government, none with the Irish government or with the Unionists. The talks may have been unofficial, but the Brits always said they would not speak to the IRA – and now they had. The end result was that the extraordinarily arrogant and politically naive IRA thought they were winning, and became even more determined to intensify the war. In response, many enraged Loyalists in the North pledged to attack as many Nationalists and Catholics as possible.

As for me, my time in prison was coming to an end, and when I was released I immediately reported for active duty to the IRA.

There was, needless to say, a world of difference between the IRA in Kerry and in Belfast. A Belfast IRA volunteer would see himself as an Irish Nationalist and Catholic, and would be motivated mainly by a fierce desire for revenge and an equally fierce determination that Northern Ireland would never return to how it had been before the civil rights movement.

Mostly I found it hard to get a proper sense from these Northern volunteers of what it meant to be discriminated against, which often seemed about not being treated with respect by the state. An IRA member south of the border might feel he had much in common with a volunteer from, say, the raw sectarian Catholic ghetto of Ardoyne in North Belfast, but his life experience was utterly different.

In Ardoyne IRA men had no problem in cheering when a 'Prod' pub was blown up and people killed. The Prods were the enemy, and always had been. Who attacked Ardoyne in 1969? The Prods. Who killed Catholics? The Prods. And who sided with the Prods? The police, the British Army and the British government. Throw in the simplistic Nationalist narrative – the uprising of 1798, the Famine, the Fenians, the executions, the Manchester martyrs, the Rising, more executions, the Black and Tans, the Treaty sell-out which had left Northern Ireland's Nationalists at the mercy of the Prods – and all that was needed was for the leadership of the Provisional IRA to supply the means.

Importantly, we also believed that our cause went back in a straight line to the Fenians, and to Pearse and Connolly; not to Parnell, Redmond or O'Connell, who had been compromisers and politicians. Ours was a cause that needed military men, men who would fight, since only this way would we gain Ireland's freedom. And fighting seemed to us a nobler way of achieving what we so desperately wanted than sly democratic means which could always be twisted and turned to suit the politicians and the Brits.

Fighting was clean and honourable, and dying for Ireland was to enjoy everlasting life, to be forever revered. A young Catholic in Ardoyne would most likely endure years of unemployment in a state he had no love for, and which in turn had little respect for him. For him, fighting would wipe away the humiliations of the past. And this time there would be no sell-out, no compromise; anything was possible in this new dawn.

In September 2014 Peter Taylor presented a BBC documentary called 'Who Won the War?' Taylor has reported and written extensively on Northern Ireland over many years. In 1974 he interviewed twelve-year-old Sean McKinley in Belfast's Divis Flats. McKinley already had the letters IRA tattooed on his knuckles.

'How do you get on with the soldiers?' Taylor asked him.

'I don't like them,' the boy replied. 'I am going to fight against them. I am going to fight for my country and DIE. Fight and DIE for Ireland.'

Forty years later Taylor found the now 52-year-old McKinley in his flat in Belfast and was visibly shocked by how he had aged. McKinley had served many years in jail for the murder of a British soldier.

Asked what advice he would give that twelve-year-old today, McKinley said, 'I would advise him to forget it, because I know a lot of people who died, and they thought they were fighting and dying for their country but it never worked out that way. It never worked out.'

There was also the added incentive that once a member was involved full time with the IRA it provided everything: food, shelter, clothes, excitement, danger. And what could be more exciting than fighting the British Army and their police in Ireland?

In June 1973 I became a full-time volunteer. My

activities in the IRA had dominated my life previously, but they moved up a notch now. It was a job that demanded my presence twenty-four hours a day, seven days a week. Always available, staying in IRA safe houses and on call at any time for whatever was required, that is how it was. I spent my days in camps in Kerry and Donegal, manufacturing explosives and homemade mortars.

In early January 1974 I went to Ballinamore in County Leitrim, where I worked in an IRA bomb factory until Easter. The work was dirty, boring, unhealthy and could be tough-going. There is nothing glamorous about working in a derelict house on a Leitrim hillside in winter and sleeping at night in a piggery, but that is what we did to produce two tonnes of homemade explosives every week.

It was a long way from *The Godfather* gangster life I sometimes read about in newspapers, and it was not a world in which there was much room for reading. Conversation was mostly about the war and its progress, and permeating everything was the sense of our invincibility and the willingness to do anything, to risk everything, to die if necessary. We had the absolute belief that we were right, and that as long as we were prepared to endure, to stick it out long enough, victory was assured. We had already won a moral victory by our willingness to fight, and no one could take that away from us.

This is not politics as understood by students of the subject or by those who would describe it as the art of the possible. This is the polar opposite. This is militarism with all its pride and purity glorifying those who fight.

In the small farms of north County Leitrim there was a strong cultural Catholicism among its people, a rough anti-clericalism when it came to politics, by which they meant the North, the IRA and the use of violence. It was not all that different from the rural, poorer parts of Kerry I knew, except that part of Leitrim bordered Northern Ireland and the reality there was more immediate and urgent. As full-time IRA volunteers we could not really be part of the local inhabitants' everyday lives, even though they fed and sheltered us. We did, however, share the same songs, stories, myths, triumphs and betrayals. Although we perceived ourselves to be at the cutting edge of the conflict, we were all part of a collective struggle for freedom, and it was our blessing, in particular as IRA volunteers, to be tasked with this noble duty.

If anyone were to ask me today how we could have fallen for all this, my answer would be, 'Easily.' People do not die, kill, go to jail, or spend their lives fighting just because it seems like a good idea. They willingly adopt a lifestyle that turns its back on material gain, and in all probability will bring nothing but hardship.

So there I was, a naive nineteen-year-old, a couple of hundred miles from home, walking up a muddy track in the freezing cold, across fields from the piggery where I had slept, to a derelict house without windows and only partially roofed, where I would spend a long day boiling fertiliser – a process which gave off stinking, noxious fumes – to make explosives that would be used to murder and maim.

The young man who walked beside me on those cold winter mornings was Kevin Coen from Riverstown in County Sligo. Less than two years later he would be shot dead by undercover soldiers as he attempted to hijack a bus near Cassidy's Cross in County Fermanagh.

Chapter 13

DISILLUSIONMENT

By spring 1974 I was in Monaghan and would shortly end up taking part in a rocket, mortar and machine-gun attack on the Deanery, a British Army and UDR base in Clogher, County Tyrone. But while I was engaged in Provisional IRA activity in East Tyrone the battle for ownership of the Connolly legacy was being bitterly fought elsewhere.

There had been tensions within the Official IRA even after the traditional militarists had formed themselves into the Provisional IRA. Within the Official IRA a group had gathered around a senior man, Seamus Costello, who saw the IRA as the defenders of Nationalists in Northern Ireland and as a liberation army fully bent on armed struggle to establish a Workers' Republic.

Costello and his associates had been agitating for the end of the Official IRA's ceasefire in Northern Ireland.

In their statement announcing the ceasefire in 1972 the Officials said that they had agreed to it because of their concern about the possibility of a sectarian civil war, which would set back for many years any prospect of a socialist revolution.

Costello was a charismatic though arrogant revolutionary who fancied himself as an Irish Che Guevara. He also talked a lot about Connolly, and believed that were Connolly alive they would both be in total agreement on the way forward: now was the time to fight, the North provided a revolutionary situation, and Republicanism was nothing if it did not fight for national freedom and socialism at the same time.* Of course, Connolly's writings are open to different interpretations, but Costello and his allies were convinced that the Official IRA had abandoned Connolly's revolutionary zeal.

Costello was expelled from the Official IRA in 1974, and then from Sinn Fein, but he and his supporters had been making plans for such an eventuality for some time. Soon a new political party was being formed, ostentatiously named the Irish Republican Socialist Party in direct mimicry of Connolly's own Irish Socialist Republican Party.

The authors Jack Holland and Henry McDonald agree: 'To the IRSP, Connolly was a beacon combining Marxist analysis with Republican credibility ... And he died from

---

* Costello was no intellectual, and his reading seemed to have been confined to a handful of Connolly's more substantial pamphlets.

the bullets of a British firing squad for asserting in arms Ireland's right to national independence ... Over the coming years he would be referred to in countless party statements and party propaganda articles, in speeches at gravesides and at Easter commemorations by IRSP spokesmen seeking to reaffirm their claim to be fighting for the kind of Ireland for which Connolly died.'[1]

The most high-profile recruit to the new party was Bernadette McAliskey, née Devlin, former MP for Mid Ulster and still regarded by many as a heroine of the civil rights movement. At the first press conference of the new organisation McAliskey said: 'The Provos are concentrating on getting rid of the British in a military campaign without any policy on the class war. And the Officials now have no policy on the national question. We will agitate on both the national and class issues.'[2] McAliskey was preaching what to her was pure Connollyism, and almost exactly what he said in the first statement after the formation of his own party twenty years before the Rising.

The IRSP first met publicly at the Spa Hotel in Lucan, County Dublin, in December 1974. There were about eighty delegates present, and they agreed that they would support a policy that the Official IRA had now rejected: a campaign of violence in Northern Ireland with the aim of forcing a British government withdrawal. There was also a strong urge, particularly in Belfast, to hit back at the Prods, and above all else a desire for action. The leadership of the Official IRA and their supporters knew that Costello had been planning to launch a military wing for some time, and they were making plans to deal with this.

Before the weekend was over some of the delegates at the conference reconvened, and the Irish National Liberation Army was born. One delegate proposed that it be called the Irish Citizen Army, and it is likely that this would have been accepted were it not that an organisation using this title had already claimed responsibility for a number of blatantly sectarian attacks, so it was felt that having two groups of the same name would cause confusion.

It was not long before the Official IRA and the INLA were at each other's throats, particularly in Belfast, though who did what to who, and where and when, is not as important as acknowledging that both were laying claim to the mantle of Connolly while murdering each other and innocent civilians. The INLA attracted criminals, disaffected Provos and Officials who joined it for a variety of reasons, some because of a closeness to a particular local leader, others because they wanted action. In their need to establish themselves quickly, as well as to protect themselves from the Official IRA, the INLA accepted near enough anyone with a pulse.

In my opinion the brutal truth is that the INLA and Seamus Costello had as much right to claim Connolly as anybody else. The IRSP believed that the Official IRA had sold out on the Nationalist side of Connolly's teaching, and the leadership of the Official IRA believed that the

IRSP were a bunch of 'Trot' ultra-leftists, sectarian gangsters and adventurers. The fact remains that after Costello was killed in Dublin in 1977, almost certainly by the Official IRA, Connolly's daughter, Nora, spoke at his graveside, and claimed that Costello was her father's true inheritor.

Once it became obvious that the INLA was the military wing of the Irish Republican Socialist Party, and that dual membership was rife, McAliskey resigned. But the INLA, fractious and often riven by internal feuding and allegations of gangsterism, survived. It went on to murder Airey Neave in the car park of the House of Commons, and three of its members would die on hunger strike in the Maze Prison, alongside seven members of the Provisional IRA in the summer of 1981. However, it was for vicious internecine feuding and brutal sectarian murder that the organisation is best known.

The Provisional IRA was not immune from the alternative that the IRSP/INLA offered. Around the time the INLA was established the Provisional IRA entered into a ceasefire with the British government that lasted about ten months. The ceasefire was not altogether popular with many Provisional IRA activists and was breached numerous times, particularly in Belfast where blatant sectarian attacks on Loyalist bars and clubs replaced the offensive against the army, police and commercial targets.

The sectarian attacks also had the advantage of keeping the IRA 'troops' busy and many very happy indeed. This ceasefire came to be regarded by most Provisional IRA members and supporters as a grave strategic mistake on the part of the leadership, then heavily under the influence of older Southerners clustered around Ruari O Bradaigh, and eventually led to their replacement by a more militant Belfast-dominated leadership.

For a brief period before they descended into chaos the INLA's militancy and their unambiguous promotion of the revolutionary socialism of Connolly was attractive to some younger Provisional IRA activists who seriously contemplated joining the new organisation. A number of those now hold very high-ranking positions in Sinn Fein.

At one stage, Costello and Brian Keenan, the most obviously Marxist of the Provisional IRA leaders, met to discuss areas of 'mutual benefit', but Costello was killed and what may have been a deadly alliance never developed. Connolly was also being mentioned much more often by people like Gerry Adams. One of his books, *The Politics of Irish Freedom*, makes many almost reverential references to Connolly; today Adams makes great play of the fact that his maternal grandfather was an associate of Connolly during his time in Belfast. Brian Keenan, a former member of the Connolly Association, and Ivor Bell, who mostly remained hidden from view inside the IRA, saw themselves as Marxists and fighters for Irish liberation, and therefore completely within the Connolly tradition.

Nothing better illustrates what became of the INLA, the organisation supposedly founded to pursue the ideals of James Connolly, than the events at the Mountain Lodge

Pentecostal Church in Darkley, County Armagh, in November 1983. As the congregation sang 'Oh, to be washed in the blood of the lamb', three armed masked men entered the small church and opened fire indiscriminately. Three church elders were murdered. Among the injured were two daughters of the pastor.

The Pentecostal Church in Ireland was founded in 1915. It predates the Rising, the partition of Ireland, the War of Independence and the Civil War. It has about 10,000 members, mostly in Northern Ireland but also in the Republic. A group calling itself the Catholic Reaction Force claimed it had carried out the attack, but no one was fooled. The weapons used were INLA guns, and the men who fired them were INLA members. In their statement they said that it was a token retaliation for the murder of Catholics by Loyalists and that they could have killed many more Protestants if they had wanted to.

It has always been the way of true believers to say that terrible things have to be done to advance the cause, and there is no doubt in my mind that Connolly preached hate, suffering, sacrifice and short cuts to the promised land.

In County Tyrone I was getting on with the daily life of a full-time active-service volunteer, which mostly meant long periods of waiting and then short and violent bursts of action. We were completely dependent for our survival on local people who fed and housed us.

The part of East Tyrone that I was based in was a large

Nationalist area where the Provisional IRA enjoyed much support, which came in various forms and was not without its limitations. Some people would do anything for us: shelter us, feed us, look after guns, whatever it took they were there; some might draw the line at us openly carrying guns in their homes; some would look the other way when they saw a couple of strangers in a neighbour's house or car; and some would drop a word if they knew the police or army were about. That there was strong support was beyond question. And that we were able to walk from safe house to safe house around the Carrickmore area in 1974 and 1975 was proof enough of that. The moderate Nationalists who did not support us mostly looked the other way too and tried to get on with their lives as best they could.

In those days my entire life revolved around the IRA. Everything was connected to the organisation whose network provided us with all that we needed, both to survive and to carry out bombing attacks against commercial targets, mainly in Cookstown and Omagh, and also, when possible, against the police and army. But we saw little of the police outside these two major towns, and if they did appear they were always accompanied by the army.

I had already taken part in the attack on the Deanery army base in Clogher, which resulted in the death of Eva Martin, a 28-year-old married schoolteacher and part-time soldier in the Ulster Defence Regiment. She was killed by an RPG-7 rocket launcher, one of a batch supplied to the Provisional IRA by Libya's Colonel Gaddafi. I was firing the mortars that night, and although none of them directly caused any injuries, I bear responsibility for her death since my purpose then was to cause as much carnage and destruction as possible. Her husband, also a part-time soldier, was on duty and stumbled over the body of his wife on a darkened staircase. I met him a number of years later and he was the most extraordinary and forgiving man. It was certainly a very humbling experience for me.

I was also involved in a number of bombings, shootings and armed robberies during this period, though none resulted in any serious injuries or fatalities. Then, around June or July of 1974, the name of Peter Flanagan, a detective inspector in the RUC Special Branch stationed in Omagh, began to be mentioned. A Catholic, born in the police station in Beragh (a small village near Omagh) where his father had been the local sergeant, Flanagan had become something of a hate figure for local Republicans, and indeed further afield. After the introduction of internment without trial in 1971, he had acquired notoriety for his supposed ill-treatment of Republican suspects in custody, although there was not a shred of evidence to back this up.

Be that as it may, at the time Flanagan was regarded as a prime target, and my order to kill him came from high up the IRA chain of command. The group put together to carry out his murder included me, Paul Norney – a seventeen-year-old IRA volunteer from Belfast who was on the run from St Patrick's Institute, from where he had escaped having been charged with the murder of a soldier – and a young Belfast woman, who was our driver. It was felt that a female driver was less likely to arouse suspicion as she waited while we walked to and from the pub through the security barriers, which were there to stop bombs being driven into Omagh's town centre.

It was known that Flanagan visited Broderick's public house in Omagh most lunchtimes during the week, always parking his blue VW Beetle a short distance away in George Street. On the morning of 23 August 1974 I hijacked a car at gunpoint from a garage in Carrickmore, telling the owner not to report it for several hours – or else. We parked the car on double yellow lines just around the corner from the security barriers, and Paul and I walked to the pub. Flanagan's car was in its usual place.

I have written about what happened next in my book *The Informer* and at length elsewhere, and it never gets any easier. I told Paul to look in and check the pub, as no one would suspect him because he looked so young and baby-faced. He opened and closed the door quickly. 'He's at the bar,' he told me.

We burst into the pub, and there was Flanagan, sitting on a stool at the bar reading the *Irish Independent*. I heard him shouting 'No' and trying to get away as we both opened fire. Flanagan stumbled and crashed through a door into the gents lavatory and we followed him in. I had fired eight shots from a Magnum and the gun was empty. He was lying on the floor, and I reloaded and shot him once more to make sure. I also reloaded because Omagh had a very large army and police presence and we had no idea who we might meet outside.

We left the pub as casually as we could and walked back to where our car was waiting. A short time later we abandoned the car on the outskirts of Omagh, got into another car and were driven to a safe house a few miles away. At 1.30 p.m. we listened to the news on the radio, which confirmed what we already knew: Peter Flanagan was dead. The voice on the radio also said that he was unmarried but had left a widowed mother. I remember thinking a most unexpected and unwelcome thought, which was: 'I'm going to have to pay for this one day.'

The next month's edition of *An Phoblacht*, the Provisional IRA's newspaper, carried a photograph of Peter Flanagan on the front page, with the headline: 'Torture Chief Shot Dead'. I felt sorry for Flanagan's mother but I had no sympathy for him; this was a war and he had chosen to fight against his own people. I felt important, invincible, heroic even, and looked up to by local supporters and other volunteers. We were hitting back, fighting the cause that the traitors had abandoned. We were special. We would do what had to be done and would not shirk from it. It was very black and white. I was living in a world of true believers who would kill and die for a holy cause that had been sanctified by the blood of our martyrs in a glorious struggle for freedom.

That time may seem very far away today, yet when I look at dissident websites and their statements and reports of meetings and commemorations it is obvious there are people, young and old, still living in a world which believes that their holy cause has been compromised and betrayed, and who will do anything to drag it back to how it once was.

It was not until early 1975, during a period of truce between the British government and the IRA, that I began to have serious doubts about the IRA's campaign. I had never been a victim of oppression or discrimination, I had not grown up under 'Orange' or British rule, and I just didn't have the real hate required. I was the product of stories and myths, a poor true believer searching for his holy cause. And yet in a way I was an idealist, repugnant to many though that thought may be. The idealist, the socialist in me, didn't want to sit around and talk with IRA volunteers and supporters about killing local farmers, teachers, shopkeepers or whoever just because they were part-time policemen or soldiers or Protestants or, like Peter Flanagan, a Catholic who had turned his back on the tribe.

Whenever I got the chance I was reading books by authors like Conor Cruise O'Brien, who had formulated a position totally opposed to the traditional simplistic Nationalist narrative. Con Houlihan, a fellow Kerryman whose writing I greatly enjoyed, was also courageously attacking the Provisional IRA publicly, and having his life threatened because of it. I was starting to realise that I'd had enough: I wanted to live. But still the ties were incredibly strong, so I decided I would talk about my doubts to Kevin McKenna, a very senior IRA man who I admired but had completely misread.

Not long after that I was in Mill Street in Monaghan town, in an IRA safe house, and Kevin McKenna was there too. I was making tea when the news reported that a policewoman had been killed in Bangor. There was a group of men watching the television, and McKenna said, 'Maybe she was pregnant and we got two for the price of one.'

I remember walking into one of the bedrooms, lying on a mattress on the floor, and crying. Shortly after this McKenna sent me to County Donegal to take over a section of the IRA based on the Donegal–Fermanagh border. Now that I was out of the Tyrone hothouse everything was calmer, and I finally made up my mind: I would go to Kerry and resign. Any member of the IRA has always been free to leave, providing they kept their mouth shut. If I had left earlier, when I was in Tyrone, the questioning about my motives would have been more intense – McKenna would have seen to that.

In October of 1975, shortly before my twenty-first birthday, I left the Provisional IRA.

I stayed in Kerry until the summer of 1976, when I went to stay with an aunt in England. Some months later I went to work in a pub in London, where I met and fell in love with the woman I would later marry. I started a small cleaning business and it was fairly successful, but

I couldn't leave bloody Ireland behind me, though I did try, believe me.

In quiet times I thought about little else, and although there was now some distance between me and the Provisional IRA's campaign, as atrocity followed atrocity, I hated myself for ever having got involved with them. I hated Ireland too, but this soon left me as I began to face the fact that no one had forced me to do what I had done. I had wanted to be special and I was, though not in the way I had perhaps intended to be. It was time to do the right thing.

I went back to Kerry in 1979, rejoined the IRA and was welcomed with open arms. Then I did what I had already decided to do: I contacted an Irish police officer and offered my services as an IRA informer. I knew what I was doing and if I had any doubts they were quickly answered by my first conversation with the IRA commander Martin Ferris shortly after my return to Ireland. Standing in Joe O'Sullivan's bar in the village of Ardfert near Tralee, I mentioned that perhaps the bombing of the La Mon House Hotel in County Down in 1978 – when twelve innocent dog-owners and breeders were burned to death by a Provisional IRA incendiary bomb – was a good example of a 'bad' operation. Ferris looked at me and said, 'I don't know what all the squealing was about. They were only Orangies anyway.' If I was looking for reassurance that becoming an informer was the right thing to do, it had just been supplied by Ferris.

The next six years were unrelenting, although working

as an informer inside the IRA didn't feel particularly dangerous to me. I was aware of the risks but it was a world I knew well; it wasn't as though I'd been sent as an agent to penetrate a foreign organisation or unknown environment I had to be taught about.

We had quite a number of successes against the IRA during this period. The capture of the *Marita Ann* off the Kerry coast with seven tonnes of weapons on board and the arrest of Ferris, now a TD for the area, was one of them. The arrests of dangerous IRA men, the seizure of weapons and the disruption of training camps – all these damaged the IRA's capacity to kill and maim. We also managed to disrupt the plan to kill Prince Charles and Princess Diana at the Dominion Theatre in London, and the parallel plan to plant sixteen bombs on English beaches in the summer of 1983. Along with that I supplied much high-grade information about the IRA and Sinn Fein's leadership plans and strategies.

By the winter of 1985 a finger of suspicion was pointing my way. My marriage had broken up, and I left Ireland with my girlfriend and five-month-old daughter on 6 December of that year. I learned later that I probably got out just in time as the IRA had decided to 'arrest' me. Whatever might have happened then would have depended on my ability to withstand heavy interrogation and keep my mouth shut, and the hope that they had no hard evidence against me.

My decision to become an informer was totally mine. Suffice to say that my family and children suffered for something that was wholly not of their knowledge or making and for which I take full responsibility. I am in my bones a selfish individual, someone who is prepared to go that extra mile when I feel I am right, and who is still capable of believing that nothing or no one matters when I have made up my mind.

Chapter 14

HUNGER STRIKES AND THE LONG WAR

For a couple of years now I have frequented a café close to the Dominion Theatre on Tottenham Court Road, where in April 1983 I was tasked by the IRA with exploring the possibility of killing Prince Charles and Princess Diana when they were due to attend a Prince's Trust charity concert later that year.

I go there to meet some friends, much younger than me, who spend their time working with young people from disadvantaged backgrounds who are at risk of getting involved in gang crime or falling through the many cracks in the system and then going on to have hopelessly unfulfilled lives.

There is no particular reason for us to meet in this café other than that it is handy for my friends, and suits me as well. I had been meeting them there for quite a while before it dawned on me how close it is to the

Dominion Theatre. Sometimes I find myself thinking about the carnage that would have resulted if a no-warning bomb had exploded near the royal box during the concert, and comparing it to the calm atmosphere in the café as I listen to the problems my friends encounter as they work passionately and intelligently to turn young people's lives around.

Mostly I can't really do much to help, but I do what I can because I know what a difference it can make to other people's lives. I also feel very privileged to contribute in some way, however small, and so fortunate to be in the position I am now in. What could possibly have been achieved by the murder of Charles and Diana? I now wonder. What purpose would have been served by doing such a terrible thing at a charity concert? How many Catholics in Northern Ireland would have died if Loyalists had carried out revenge attacks? Would they have bombed Dublin in retaliation? Would there have been a reaction against Irish people living in Britain?

I thought at the time that the plan was stupid and brutal in its concept, and I am glad I was able to make sure it never happened. And sitting here in this café on this busy London street, alongside people who love life and want to expand it, who want to build and not destroy, and who transmit this joy to all who know them, I am thankful that I am no longer surrounded by hate and anger or by the fanaticism of true believers.

*   *   *

The movement I had joined in 1970 was small, badly trained and poorly equipped, but it embodied a history and a tradition of violent resistance to British rule in Ireland. It was reflective of what Fearghal McGarry describes as, 'A distinctive political tradition rooted more in an incoherent blend of Fenianism, Catholic nationalism and Irish cultural nationalism than the Republican principles of the American or French revolutions.'[1] I have thought long and hard about how to describe that tradition, and this is as good a description as one is likely to get.

We were also at the beginning of a period that was to be called – in that way we Irish have of avoiding reality – the Troubles, and it was impossible then to imagine the horror, the killings, the ruined lives and the quarter-century and more of unrelenting violence that would see over 3,000 people die in these islands and in Europe, most of them innocent civilians. The war I was about to become involved in was indeed a Long War, a strategy that was first endorsed in the mid-1970s by such people as Gerry Adams, Brian Keenan and Ivor Bell in the Provisional IRA, who had worked out that if the war was to be successful it was going to take a very long time. These three individuals, along with Martin McGuinness, were the chief architects of this strategy, although in the public mind it is most associated with or credited to Gerry Adams.

Until 1975 every year was going to be the year of victory, and when that nonsense stopped it was replaced by a strategy that paid no regard to the suffering it would inevitably inflict on the people of Northern Ireland. Like the 1916 leaders who did not have the foresight to see that it would be the inhabitants of Dublin's slums who would suffer disproportionately, Adams, Keenan, Bell and McGuinness also failed to understand that it would be the inhabitants of those enclaves in Belfast and Derry where they had most support who would carry much of the burden of their Long War. Or maybe they just didn't care. Perhaps Sean O'Casey summed it up best in his 1923 play *The Shadow of a Gunman*: 'I object to the gunmen dying for the people when the people are dying for the gunmen.'[2]

Therefore, in the same way that Connolly's blood-bonding of Nationalism with socialism is seen by some as his genius, we can draw a comparison with Adams as the brains behind the IRA's Long War strategy; this was his political genius. There are other words that come to my mind in both cases, and genius is not one of them. Even as far back as 1975 I would hear some Republicans, usually older ones, say that the war had gone on for too long.

By late 1975 my thinking was that our war had been wrongly conceived from the start, and we did not deserve to win it. A Long War fought and supported by people who depended on the enemy for housing, social welfare and infrastructure was a war that the state could manipulate. Settling into the rhythm of a low-intensity campaign in such circumstances demanded a high sacrifice from a relatively small number of IRA supporters who were more vulnerable to attack from Loyalists than the activists were. I was also concerned that these supporters, and particularly the people who merely lived in the affected areas, were going to get it in the neck every day, week, month and year that the war continued. As innocent Catholics became victims of loyalist attacks, the more they depended on the IRA for protection it could not deliver: it could only retaliate for Loyalist attacks, not protect against them.

Support the IRA or not, people who lived in the Republican heartlands such as North and West Belfast, Derry, East Tyrone and South Armagh were daily participants in this war. Caught between the IRA, the Loyalists, the British Army and the police, the pressure on everyday life was relentless and grim.

The price to be paid for this Long War in Nationalist areas alone has yet to be properly reckoned, but already surveys and studies are showing that the damage to mental health in the form of suicide, marriage breakdown, juvenile crime, drug abuse, alcoholism and domestic violence is truly shocking.

And throughout this barbarity, as condemnation rained down on their heads from every quarter, the IRA claimed the legitimacy of their struggle came from the 'men of 1916'. Over and over again they stated, 'If they were right, we are right.' Words and phrases from the Proclamation and from the writings and speeches of Pearse and Connolly were used to prove that they were the rightful inheritors; the moral guardians of the betrayed republic. If the martyrs of 1916 were right, how could this generation be wrong? How could Bobby Sands be a criminal? Or as Connolly put it in the last words he wrote before his execution, and which were smuggled out by his daughter: 'Believing that the British government has no right in Ireland, never had any right in Ireland and never can have any right in Ireland, the presence, in any one generation of Irishmen, of even a respectable minority, ready to die to affirm that truth, makes that Government for ever a usurpation and a crime against human progress.'[3].

In her book *We Shall Rise Again* Nora Connolly writes: 'I'll just tell you what my father said ... And the Provisionals were all very touched, and they clapped and clapped. "We shall rise again," I said, "and we have risen. This is the continuation – so that the tradition has not been broken. Here we are rising again. And if we go down, we'll rise again!"'[4]

There are too many people who are still prepared to say that the Provisional IRA was a legitimate organisation, with a long historic narrative and a story to tell that reeks of injustice, famine and oppression. It is a story, or at least a version of it, that has gone around the world, but I for one do not recognise it.

When I came back to Ireland and rejoined the Provisional IRA in 1979, this time voluntarily working for the Irish police, the IRA was not in a healthy position. Weapons, money and quality recruits were scarce, and support north and south of the border and in Irish America was slowly but steadily ebbing away. It was an organisation that had been at war for almost ten years, and the jails were pretty full. Bloody Friday, Kingsmill, Birmingham, casual murder upon murder and bomb upon bomb had literally blown away much of the romantic nonsense associated with the desire for a united Ireland.

After the killing by explosion of eight Republican prisoners at Ballyseedy Cross by Free State soldiers during the Civil War in the early 1920s, a short distance from where I was born, it was said that the crows were eating flesh from the trees for days afterwards. The same could surely be said of the innumerable IRA atrocities in the 1970s, 1980s, 1990s, and since. The war was continuing, the IRA would have occasional successes, and sometimes spectacular ones, but mainly it was bleak stuff all round.

The public language of the IRA during the late 1970s had also become much more socialist and anti-imperialist in tone. After the murder of Lord Mountbatten in 1979 the IRA statement claiming responsibility included the words: 'We will tear out your soft imperialist heart.' This uncompromising rhetoric owed much to what is often, but not quite accurately, described as the new leadership of Adams, Bell, Keenan and McGuinness, and reflected the ideological Marxism of Keenan and Bell as well as the left-leaning incoherent Fenianism of their comrades, along with a good old dollop of solid sectarianism.

References to Connolly were far more frequent in the discourse of the Provisional IRA in the late 1970s and 1980s, but perhaps the greatest relevance he had to Belfast

Nationalists was that the Sinn Fein head office was called Connolly House. It became notorious throughout the Troubles as the place where children and adults were told to report to when they were to be punished for 'anti-social' activities. This Sinn Fein centre, Connolly House in Andersonstown, was also repeatedly referred to as a co-ordinating centre for punishment attacks on children and adults in West Belfast.[4]

The prison protests that began in 1976 when the government decided to end Special Category Status for political prisoners have been described by that generation of militant Irish Republicans as 'our 1916'. Without these protests or the subsequent hunger strikes it is very likely that the Long War would have hit the rocks well before it did.

The protests started when Republican prisoners refused to wear prison uniforms, and so ended up confined to their cells wearing only blankets. The protest escalated in 1978 as prisoners began smearing their own excrement on cell walls. The first hunger strike in 1980 ended in confusion, with the prisoners believing the government had agreed to their demands. It was soon obvious that any agreement was open to different interpretations and that the authorities had the whip hand.

By the time Bobby Sands began the second hunger strike on 1 March 1981 it was made absolutely clear, so as to avoid any repeat of the confusion surrounding the ending of the first hunger strike, that final authority would rest with the leadership of the Republican movement, meaning the IRA Army Council. Communications with the prisoners would be handled by Republican leaders such as Gerry Adams and others who lived in Belfast and were in daily contact with the strikers and their families and supporters. This would allow for decisions to be made at short notice. It was this group based in Belfast who would also handle contact and negotiations with outside agencies, the British government and the prison authorities, although everything possible had to be done to maintain the fiction that the prisoners themselves had autonomy in the matter of beginning or ending their hunger strikes.

The whole dynamic of the hunger strike changed when Frank Maguire, the Independent Republican MP for Fermanagh and South Tyrone, died of a heart attack. After some dithering and arm-twisting, Bobby Sands was put forward as a popular-front, Nationalist, Catholic, IRA hunger-strike candidate, and was duly elected as MP for the area.

There is now much controversy about what precisely happened during the 1981 hunger strikes. Among others, Richard O'Rawe, the prisoners' public relations officer in the Maze prison, has said – in his book *Blanketmen** – that the IRA leadership spurned the opportunity to end the strike after the fourth hunger striker

* The entire book is about whether or not a deal was possible. O'Rawe is emphatic that it was, and that it was scuppered by the outside leadership.

died. Did the leadership in Belfast, who were primarily responsible for co-ordination with the prisoners, let at least six of the hunger strikers die needlessly just to enhance Sinn Fein's electoral support?

When historians try to make such events neat and tidy they often gloss over the intense emotion, the conflicts of interest, the desire by all parties not to be fooled or sold short, and the IRA's ambition to exploit the situation for maximum gain. What else would one expect them to do? But Adams and the IRA and Sinn Fein leadership were not experienced negotiators and had stumbled into the full glare of international publicity. Many of them knew the hunger strikers, their families, friends and supporters. But they also knew that a by-election following the death of Sands was pending, that Irish-American support had been galvanised, that money was pouring in, that a street in Tehran had been renamed after Sands, and that Gaddafi, after losing interest in Ireland for a while, was broadcasting messages of support on Libyan radio. So the leadership dithered, over-negotiated and finally let their comrades die because it broadly seems to me that it better suited their purpose that way.

The hunger strikers died for not much more than was on offer after the first strike ended, and my feeling then and now is that the IRA leadership could have asked the prisoners to end their strikes. It would have, in effect, been an order that would have been obeyed by the prisoners.

I also knew that the IRA and Sinn Fein leadership

was so desperate to pretend the ending of the hunger strike was a matter for the prisoners involved that they simply would not instigate the decision. As was proved throughout the IRA campaign, every time the IRA leaders had a hard call to make they ducked it and called for more sacrifice from their members, which meant that more died. This was compounded by the fact that Southern Nationalists had once again turned squeamish and wanted it all to go away. I know this to be true, having heard and witnessed it everywhere I went in the South. It was also reflected in the serious drop in attendance at protest meetings as the death toll from the street violence rose, and the prisoners and their families and many others suffered an agonising wait for news. Increasingly people began to call for an act of humanity from the IRA leadership, but none was forthcoming.

Contrast this with the action of Arthur Griffith, the founder of Sinn Fein, another 'grey man' and a strong supporter of the Anglo-Irish Treaty of 1921. After the death on hunger strike of Terence MacSwiney in Brixton Prison in 1920, and two other IRA prisoners on hunger strike in Cork Prison, and with nine others remaining in serious danger of dying, Griffith – then acting president of the Republic – made the following appeal to the men still on hunger strike: 'I am of the opinion that our countrymen in the Cork prison have sufficiently proved their devotion and fidelity and they should now, as they were prepared to die for Ireland, prepare to live for her.'

In September of 1981 I remember being asked by Mr and

Mrs Mullan from Altamuskin, County Tyrone – whose home I often stayed in in the 1970s, and whose son, Pat, had recently joined the hunger strike – if I could do anything to bring it to an end. The conversation took place in the Hotel Imperial in Dundalk prior to a National Anti H-Block meeting. They were fiercely committed Republicans (their other son would later be shot dead by the British Army), but they did not want Pat to die in a protest that was so obviously going nowhere. I had no influence over these decisions but said I would pass it on.

Many innocent people were also killed during this period in Northern Ireland, but perhaps one incident illustrates the grim reality of those terrible times. Immediately after the death of Sands at 1.17 a.m. on 5 May 1981, a mentally-disabled man carried away by the excitement of the rioting took part in the stoning of a milk float which crashed and killed the driver and his fifteen-year-old son. Innocent people were dying as Republican leaders like Adams basked in the glow of a media spotlight which even months before they could not have imagined and would certainly have killed for.

I sometimes ask myself what the difference is between a suicide bomber and a hunger striker, and how much all this resembles the blood sacrifice of Connolly and Pearse in 1916. In the end, it is about a belief system, an ideology. Connolly found his in Marxism and was completely loyal to it, so loyal that he sacrificed everything, and would willingly have sacrificed everyone he loved for it.

He would, I think, have approved of the hunger strikes that unleashed a wave of Catholic Nationalism throughout Ireland. From May until October of 1981 the Rosary, the prayers, the holy water, every weapon in the Irish Catholic cultural arsenal made its appearance on the streets of Ireland, north and south of the border, and in the prisons where the communal recitation of the Rosary, often twice a day, became commonplace among the prisoners. No public meeting or gathering in the summer of 1981 seemed complete without prayers and reference to Calvary and Jesus on the cross, and to the executed heroes of the Rising. Black flags fluttered from lampposts and windows in many towns and villages as the entire martyrdom complex was allowed free range.

It seemed extraordinary to me that there could be so much sympathy for the hunger strikers in Nationalist Ireland, among people who under normal circumstances would have said they hated the Provisional IRA. Yet somehow they had persuaded themselves that in the case of the hunger strikes this did not apply. Again it must be emphasised that the vast majority of people acknowledged what they saw as the bravery and sacrifice of the hunger strikers and then quickly went about their business. This was not support for the activities of the Provisional IRA as such, but more indicative of a kind of cognitive disorder in the Irish Nationalist psyche.

The IRA was also careful to pick hunger strikers who

had not been convicted of particularly brutal or overtly sectarian incidents. It would not have made good PR sense in the South of Ireland or indeed internationally to have to explain why a man who had thrown a no-warning bomb into a Protestant bar was now being canonised in the Nationalist consciousness as another Pearse or Connolly.

Were the hunger strikers true believers? Certainly they were prepared to lay down their lives for a holy cause. The second hunger striker to die, Frank Hughes from Bellaghy in County Derry, made no bones about how he saw it. In a message (which I have read) smuggled out of the prison he made it clear that owing to the injuries he had suffered before being captured he could never escape from prison and was therefore of not much use to the IRA. He was joining the hunger strike, not because he wanted to be treated as a Special Category prisoner, or prisoner of war, but because he needed to do what he still could to advance the cause.

Frank Hughes had no doubt that he would die, and wanted to make sure that his death would result in more recruits, more dead soldiers and policemen, and ultimately contribute to victory. He knew he was committing suicide and, as he and the IRA were well aware, that it was a mortal sin for Catholics, so the farce had to be kept up that the hunger strike and his impending death were really about the prisoners' demand to be treated as POWs. It was partly about this, but fundamentally it was about exploiting the blood of the martyrs to legitimise the Long War. The awesome power of the martyr sacrifice with its religious, cultural and ethnic resonance had once again come back to haunt us.

When Monsignor Denis Faul – a man who courageously stood out against the Provisional IRA but also condemned Loyalist murders and excesses by the British security forces – tried to persuade Sands to end his strike, Sands simply said, 'Greater love hath no man than to lay down his life for his friends.' It was Faul who later facilitated the families of hunger strikers to intervene when the strikers were near death, thus ending the strike and earning him the lasting enmity of the IRA leadership.

Two months before his death, Sands wrote in his diary, on 9 March 1981: 'I always keep thinking of James Connolly ... Connolly has always been the man that I look up to.'[6]

Chapter 15

RELEASE

I had been thinking of handing myself in for some time, but it was not until 1988 that I finally decided to come clean. I walked into an English police station and admitted to my IRA activities in the mid-1970s. I was brought back to Northern Ireland and just over a year later was sentenced to life imprisonment.

I was released in 1996 under a royal prerogative of mercy. After my release I found myself thrown into a bit of a publicity firestorm, or at least that was what it felt like for someone with no experience of media attention.

The IRA had declared a ceasefire in August 1994, to much celebration in Republican areas and a wave of relief in Nationalist Ireland and further afield. However, many Unionists in Northern Ireland were wary of the ceasefire, if not downright hostile, and feared a secret deal between the IRA and the British government. As for me, I seriously doubted the ceasefire would last, but was fairly certain that we were entering the final stages of the Provisional IRA's violent campaign to force Unionists into a united Ireland against their will.

In reality, the Provisional IRA's apparent change of heart was more a change of strategy brought about by necessity. The Irish Republic had become sickened by the Long War and everything pertaining to the North, which was now a byword for brutality and horror. Gerry Adams had lost his West Belfast seat in the general election of 1992, and Sinn Fein regarded it a success if one of their candidates saved their deposit when they contested an election in the South. Many of their most experienced operators were in jail; their core support was exhausted and frightened of Loyalist murder gangs, who had stepped up their activity. The IRA may have been able to continue their campaign, but the cost of maintaining it was prohibitive. Their supporters might be cheered up by the occasional 'spectacular', but Adams, McGuinness and their more astute associates knew the reality: they were facing political irrelevance and ultimate defeat.

This was not how everyone in the IRA saw it, and as always there were those who were keen to remain pure and unsullied by politics. Under huge internal pressure, but also confident through the soundings they had taken that the Labour government-in-waiting would prove more amenable than the present Conservative government, the

Adams–McGuinness leadership decided the time had come to act.

The IRA ceasefire ended on 9 February 1996 with a huge explosion at Canary Wharf in London that killed two civilians. From then on the campaign stumbled on in a half-hearted and ineffectual manner as the IRA waited for the new Labour government led by Tony Blair to be elected in May 1997. The organisation was treading water, though this still resulted in several dead and injured civilians, policemen, soldiers, and the arrest and imprisonment of quite a few of their members. By now most of its leadership were looking for a way out, but a way out that would allow them to snatch as much as possible from the jaws of defeat.

There are many people who believe that Adams and McGuinness enjoyed complete hegemony over the Provisional IRA during this period, but that was untrue. They carried considerable weight, to be sure, and were determined to go down a certain road. They had also prepared well over the past several years, and proved very adept at outwitting their internal opponents.

I hit a bit of controversy in those early days and many people questioned my motives and credibility. I was accused of being against peace because Adams and McGuinness had now become the 'peace people', and anyone who doubted their intentions was immediately dubbed anti-peace and clubbed over the head, metaphorically at least. I did not give any serious consideration to this, although it brought back unhappy memories of the anti-Nationalist charge that was frequently used to stifle any dissent in the Ireland I grew up in.

There was another controversy that became a major issue after I was released in 1996 and caused me a lot of soul-searching, which was the murder by the Provisional IRA of Corkman Sean Corcoran in 1985. Corcoran had become involved with the Provisionals in the mid-1970s in Cork City. When he was arrested by the police he admitted his involvement but was not charged on condition that he report back on local IRA activists. He did this for some time until various IRA members became unsure of him, although this was more because they thought he was weak and unreliable rather than any concrete evidence. By late 1983 there was a change in the local IRA leadership, which was when I first met Corcoran. I was immediately disturbed by him, perhaps for subliminal reasons I have never been able to articulate, and I made it clear to the Garda officer I worked with that I was convinced he was an informer and extremely vulnerable. Although he never confirmed my suspicions.

Then Corcoran began to do all sorts of dangerous things: he phoned the Sinn Fein centre in Tralee to ask for a meeting with me, he claimed to others that he had a high-level contact in Irish army intelligence who was giving him information, and generally behaved erratically. I pleaded on numerous occasions with my Garda officer that they move Corcoran and his family or he would end up in real trouble. I could protect him for a while, I told the Garda, but not for ever.

Eventually Corcoran came to the attention of the IRA's internal security department. When he was kidnapped and immediately admitted to being an informer, I was tasked with bringing his taped confession to Pat Doherty, a member of the IRA's Army Council, senior member of Sinn Fein and MP for West Tyrone. I was hopeful that I could persuade him to produce Corcoran at a press conference and embarrass the police and Irish government, but Doherty was having none of it, I suspect mainly because he wanted to enhance his own credentials as a hardliner. He instructed me to bring the confession tape to Kevin McKenna, now chief of staff of the Provisional IRA. I did and tried once again to persuade him to call a press conference, but McKenna vetoed this and ordered Corcoran's murder.

I had made numerous attempts to convince my Garda contact that Corcoran was about to be killed, but it was all to no avail. Maybe because I had managed to save people before in somewhat similar circumstances, I could not seem to get it across that I had effectively lost control over this situation. I also told my contact where I thought Corcoran was being held, but still the Gardai did nothing. Eventually Sean Corcoran was murdered by members of the IRA's internal security department and his body dumped on the roadside outside Cork City.

Corcoran's murder was a terrible tragedy for him and his family, and yet another sickening result of the so-called glorious Long War.

*   *   *

Shortly after I was released in 1996 I got to know David Trimble, the leader of the Ulster Unionist Party. I liked him, and still do. I met him quite a few times in the years leading up to the Belfast Agreement,* though, contrary to media comment and speculation, I was never an adviser to him. I spoke with him a lot and may have occasionally helped to clarify a few thoughts or tweak something. But I believed then and I believe now that David Trimble is his own man, a very intelligent man, who always had a clear idea of where the process was going. He wanted the violence to end and an accommodation reached between Nationalist and Unionist, North and South, Britain and Ireland, but only within the context of preserving the United Kingdom of Great Britain and Northern Ireland. This, in his view, was the only worthwhile deal in town, and it was – with a few stickers and bells attached to keep Sinn Fein happy – essentially the constitutional deal that was arrived at.

However, it is true to say that for many people in Ireland, not just the Unionists, it stank. I supported it but honestly there were times when I too was disgusted by it. Blair and some of his advisers, though I exclude Peter Mandelson, seemed to have little sense of the dangers in negotiating with a so-called political party whose leadership was still involved with an active terrorist

---

* I prefer not to call it the Good Friday Agreement, which is not its proper title but a media invention that keys into pseudo-religious overtones.

organisation (the Provisional IRA), and their immersion in group-think peacemaking meant they were soon in danger of speaking the same language as Adams and McGuinness.

Much of the peace process – though not the constitutional agreement, which was a huge defeat for the Provisional IRA – was not only suspect but also destructive of the democratic norms on the island of Ireland. How all this will yet play out we do not know, but sometimes it seems as if the effect of Blair's casual disregard for the detail of the democratic process has left gaping holes in the accountability in Northern Ireland, and undermined the same in the Irish Republic, with both governments creating some unpleasant precedents. For example, John Hume's party, the SDLP, had much more electoral support than Sinn Fein, but simply because they did not have any guns their opinions were often bypassed in the latter stages of the talks. We did the right thing, I am sure of this, but I am still concerned that too many British politicians became carried away in the excitement and drama of dealing with terrorists, and their glamorisation of people like Adams and McGuinness as near mythological peacemakers still causes distress and hurt to many people in Ireland, not just the Unionists.

In my opinion, if any man can be said to have taken risks for peace it was David Trimble, both in respect to his career (he lost his parliamentary seat) and indeed to his own life. So I supported him because we had a commonality of purpose, but I was not in any way crucial or important to the deal that eventually emerged.

Later I had several meetings in Belfast with a senior member of the Loyalist Ulster Volunteer Force in an effort to persuade them to decommission their weapons. They did eventually, although they did it in their own time and I doubt if my input made much difference. I also talked with a lot of politicians, mostly Irish, British and American, and with Loyalist paramilitaries, academics, members of the Orange Order, all sorts of people from all over the place, including Jonathan Powell, the prime minister's chief of staff, who handled the daily grind of the negotiations. It was a whirlwind time, during which I was very much a target for the IRA, and both then and later a number of plans were made to kill me, but for sensible reasons I believe that the details are best left with the police.

My relationship with the IRA was not helped when I gave evidence in Dublin in a libel case brought in 1998 by Thomas 'Slab' Murphy, then the IRA's chief of staff, against the *Sunday Times* for alleging that he was an IRA leader involved in cross-border smuggling and other terrorist activities. Slab Murphy turned up in court and posed as an innocent farmer, but the weight of the combined testimony against him soon demolished his pretence. His supporters from South Armagh invaded the Four Courts in Dublin as the trial went on. Looking like something out of *The Sopranos*, they arrived in flash cars with mobile phones, and they wandered around making full use of the citizen's right of access to all public parts of the courts. They were there to intimidate, but the Irish Republic had moved on, and while these men could certainly scare they could not bully the metropolitan Dublin jury, who just looked at them in bewilderment. It was a fairly fraught experience for all those involved,* but thankfully Murphy lost the case, which was not just a great victory for the *Sunday Times* and its lawyers but also for Irish democracy.

That it was life-threatening to face down the Provisional IRA was brutally confirmed when on 27 January 1999 the badly mutilated body of former IRA man Eamon Collins was discovered on a road in Newry, County Down. Collins had publicly criticised the IRA, and his autobiography *Killing Rage* had been published to much critical acclaim. He too had given evidence against Slab Murphy in the same trial. The coroner and state pathologist agreed that it was one of the most brutal, grotesque and horrific murders they had ever encountered. The coroner said that 'sub-human thugs' had carried out the murder, and the policeman in charge of the investigation said that he believed the Provisional IRA in South Armagh were responsible.

Some IRA members, including fairly senior people, had long been unhappy at what they saw as the political

---

* Not least for me, though I tried not to think about it too much as the release of my autobiography, *The Informer*, would take place a week or so later.

direction in which Adams, McGuinness and their supporters were taking the organisation. In spite of this, on 19 July 1997 the IRA had reinstated their ceasefire. On 29 August the British government had invited Sinn Fein into the Stormont peace talks, and on 9 September Sinn Fein had pledged to abide by the Mitchell Principles, as formulated by the American senator George Mitchell. Senator Mitchell had taken on the role of chairing the talks at Stormont Castle that would result in the Belfast Agreement, thereby committing those parties who signed up to the Principles to solving the crisis by exclusively peaceful means. Three members of the IRA Army Council were among the Sinn Fein delegation that signed up, and this was the final straw for a group of dissidents who regarded them as having breached the IRA constitution.

The group was led by Mickey McKevitt, a senior IRA quartermaster and member of the IRA Executive.* McKevitt and his supporters, four of them also members of the Executive, made one last attempt to get control of the IRA. But at an IRA convention on the weekend of 10 September, McKevitt and his supporters were outvoted and comprehensively outwitted by the Adams–McGuinness leadership. To be honest, it was no contest as the dissidents had left it way too late to make their

---

* The IRA Executive consists of a twelve-member body, which is elected at a convention and from which the seven-man IRA Army Council is formed.

move, and Adams and McGuinness had been persuading potential and actual dissidents to support them for quite some time. McKevitt may have been a competent IRA quartermaster but he was relatively unknown and in comparison to Adams and McGuinness he was a light-weight. The really serious dissidents had either already left the movement, been expelled or remained and chose, for whatever reasons, to stay with Adams and McGuinness.

McKevitt and his supporters therefore decided to reconstitute the IRA; to their minds their former comrades were no longer bona fide Republicans. They reconvened, elected a new leadership and reaffirmed their position as the lawful government of Ireland and their authority to use whatever means they saw fit to establish their Republic. The existence of the split became obvious to the outside world with the announcement of the forma-tion of the 32 County Sovereignty Committee in Dublin on 7 December 1997,* which went on to become the public face of the newly formed Real IRA.

In effect, the dissidents were once again demonstrating the loathing of a core section of extreme Irish Nationalism for 'politics', a sort of shorthand for a hatred of the liberal state – a hatred they share with all political and religious fanatics. Adams and McGuinness had sold out, just as Michael Collins, Eamon de Valera and Cathal Goulding

---

* Its best-known founding member carried a name that had huge cachet for Republicans. Bernadette Sands McKevitt was a sister of Bobby Sands, and was also married to Mickey McKevitt.

had before them. They had flirted with the evil of politics and been seduced. It is always the same sick story: the inadequate and malcontent huddling together under the blanket cover of purity, and spitting their rage at a world that will not behave in the way they want it to.

It was not long before the Real IRA made their intentions clear with a number of car bombs in mostly Unionist-populated towns within striking distance of South Armagh and North Louth, where McKevitt and much of his support was based. They also carried out mortar attacks on army bases in the same area. Well versed in how to handle splits in their party, the Provisional IRA moved quickly to dissuade members from joining or helping this new and dangerous group. But it was a time of shifting alliances, and some IRA members, though not overtly willing to support the Real IRA, were prepared to lend a quiet hand when it suited them.

Then, in Omagh, County Tyrone, on 15 August 1998, long after most people thought the worst of the violence was over, what could have been just another car bomb exploded with devastating consequences. The 15th of August is celebrated in the Roman Catholic calendar as the Feast of the Assumption of the Virgin Mary into Heaven, and has traditionally been a day of Mass and celebratory parades. It is also traditionally a day when mothers and children shop for school uniforms before the start of the new school year. It was also carnival day in Omagh and the streets were bustling with various entertainments. Shoppers and people from the town and surrounding area were enjoying themselves in the sunshine and the relaxed atmosphere.

At 2.29 p.m., a caller using a recognised Real IRA code word said that a 500-pound car bomb would explode in Omagh Main Street in thirty minutes – there is no Main Street in Omagh. Several other calls followed but they proved to be equally misleading, partly because the bombers were hopelessly inefficient and did not know the town. But they did know that carnival day would be an easy opportunity to drive into Omagh and park the car unnoticed. The fact that the town was heaving with people either did not cross their minds or did not bother them.

Here is the difficult part for me: I planted bombs in Omagh, but fortunately they never killed or injured anyone, although they did damage homes and property. And as I have written earlier, bombs are unpredictable, especially the homemade variety. I know full well that the bombs I brought to Omagh could have slaughtered people, and when I think about it now I know there is no excuse for what I did as a young man.

The bomb exploded at 3.04 p.m., and because of the confused warnings many people were moved or directed by police closer to the bomb rather than further way. Twenty-nine people and two unborn babies died, and around 300 were injured. As well as being horrific for everyone caught up in it, the bombing was also a disaster for the Real IRA. Revulsion and condemnation poured in from everywhere. McKevitt and his wife came under direct pressure from local people in Dundalk, where they lived and owned a small print shop. The Real IRA declared a ceasefire three days later, but as the months went by and only one man was charged in connection with the bombing it began to appear that if the Real IRA could lie low for a while they might ride it out, and even in time resume their campaign.

Then some of the victims' relatives came up with the idea of suing the suspected bombers in a civil court. It had never been done before, but a solicitor called Jason McCue was more than keen to take on the case. McCue had visited me in prison in connection with other terrorist cases he was working on and was now a good friend. Over the next few years, and I must admit reluctantly at first, I became very involved in their campaign. I was reluctant because of my background and how the victims and relatives might react to me, but also because I did not want to provide sensationalist copy for the media. But we managed to overcome most of this and I helped out wherever I was useful. After a considerable amount of work by the many people involved in the campaign, the case against McKevitt and four others finally opened in Belfast High Court on 7 April 2008. Following some unbelievably frustrating proceedings, including in the Dublin courts, judgement was delivered in Belfast High Court on 8 June 2009.

Mr Justice Morgan held that the Army Council of the Real IRA bore responsibility for organising the bombing, he found McKevitt and three of the four defendants responsible for the bomb, and he awarded aggravated damages to those victims who had brought the case. The judgement would never bring back the relatives' loved ones, but it was a vindication of all they had been through, and the process could be used again whenever the state failed to prosecute in terrorist cases. Perhaps one of the most important things about the campaign was its fundraising, which heightened awareness around the globe and meant that the Real IRA could never crawl out from under the stone of Omagh. No matter what the organisation did, the victims' families pursued them relentlessly and imaginatively at every opportunity. Enormous credit is due to everyone who stuck with what was an incredibly harrowing experience. Proceedings are still ongoing to trace Real IRA assets and force McKevitt and his associates to disclose any personal assets. At the time of writing, a number of court hearings are ongoing.

Long after the second and final Provisional IRA ceasefire was declared on 19 July 1997, the IRA was still kneecapping, mutilating, occasionally murdering, robbing banks and smuggling, all to control and finance their political operation. This was common knowledge then, and it remains common knowledge now. Owing to the murky realm that is the IRA, it is hard to know with absolute certainty whether they have yet stopped these activities.

Deep suspicion is attached to the activities of well-known IRA members in the South Armagh area, where enormous sums of money are still raised through smuggling.

Knowing the type of people involved, I doubt the money exclusively fills their own pockets, but it is no coincidence that Sinn Fein enjoys resources way beyond any other political party on the island. The same people who directed the brutality and slaughter for years now run Sinn Fein, and I for one am deeply suspicious of their strategy and motives. Of course people change, of course redemption is possible, but they have not displayed one iota of genuine regret for the terrible things they have done. Instead they lecture those who've never murdered, terrorised, robbed, cheated or lied, about the need for probity, transparency in public life, honesty and justice. To me, this is to live in a world where wrong is right and right is wrong.

Personally, I will do whatever I can to ensure that Sinn Fein never gains political power in the Irish Republic. I don't believe they have anything to offer except anger and hate, as well as the terrifying prospect that young Loyalists in Northern Ireland will see what is happening in the Republic and believe they will once again be under siege. Listening to politicians and people from the Republic talk about peace while the electorate merrily goes out to vote for Sinn Fein, the only all-Ireland party aggressively campaigning for Irish unity, is not going to persuade Unionists of anything except the need for fear and suspicion.

The year 2016 sees the centenary of the Easter Rising, and tensions in Northern Ireland will inevitably rise. The various dissident IRA groups, who all believe they are

James Connolly's disciples, will try and take advantage of this. The fastest-growing dissident group in Northern Ireland did not call themselves the 1916 Societies without reason.

I now spend some of my time working with young people at risk of becoming involved in extremism or violent crime. I don't belong to any particular organisation or group, I just get around when and where I can and work quietly with some of these projects.

When considering fanaticism, I am still often amazed at the way some so-called experts treat it as a phenomenon that is somehow 'other', as if fanaticism can have an existence of its own, divorced from our core individuality. In 1951, the moral and social philosopher Eric Hoffer wrote: 'There are vast differences in the content of holy causes and doctrines, but a certain uniformity in the factors which make them effective.'[1] He went on to say, in words that are timeless: 'The True Believer is everywhere on the march, and both by converting and antagonising he is shaping the world in his own image. And whether we are to line up with him or against him, it is well that we should know all we can concerning his nature and potentialities.'[2]

Everyone I have introduced to *The True Believer* finds it a disturbing book because it looks right into our hearts and asks penetrating questions about our deepest motivations.

During the 2015 British general election, Anjem

Choudary, the London-based Islamist preacher, and his associates handed out leaflets stating that to vote in an election is a great sin against God, and that democracy is a sinful challenge to God's will. Choudary also preaches that there is no concept of freedom of expression in Islam.

Like the vast majority in our society I hold diametrically opposing views, but too often we take the beauty of liberal democracy for granted. It is gentle by its very nature and does not easily answer to calls to the barricade. But unless we first call a spade a spade and lose our fear of words we will continue to delude ourselves as to the nature of fanaticism, and we will never even begin to grapple with the problem coherently.

During a short break while writing this I picked up the *Spectator* magazine (4 July edition, 2015) only to be greeted with the following opening line in the editorial: 'That democracy is a superior form of government to any other goes without saying.' Does it really? An awful lot of the world disagrees with this statement, so maybe it does need saying in very clear terms. After all, it is largely the belief system we subscribe to that defines how we live our lives. There is no need to invent a special language when talking about fanaticism. I know where I stand, which is on the side of liberal democracy, which is imperfect, it has to be, but will only be improved, to the benefit of real people, by debate, discussion and not by revolution, murder and mayhem in the pursuit of the Holy Cause, whether that be the extermination of the Jewish people, the Caliphate, the Workers' Republic of Connolly, or the 'pure' Gaelic Ireland of the ultra-Irish Nationalist.

But what of Connolly and other true believers who have infected our history, and still excite some who believe their word sacred? Vaclav Havel issues a warning: 'I have nothing against historical parallels and meditations on the tendencies of our national history … it only bothers me when they are used to distract our attention from the living, human, moral and political dilemmas of the time, for, if we were to solve or deal with these, we would be making our own national history and ultimately giving it some kind of meaning.'[3]

It remains the case that many people would like to see me dead. Memories live long in Ireland, and nowhere more than in the realm of extreme Irish Nationalism, where hatred for the informer runs deep. But as I now look back on it all, at my early days when I worshipped Connolly, when I was working for a cause I believed in, I realise how easy it is to buy into a community of victimhood.

The legends and stories of community grievance are always about humiliation. Across the Muslim world today the story told is one of centuries of humiliation at the hands of the West, the Christian, the Crusader, the Jew. In Ireland and in the Edinburgh slum in which James Connolly grew up, it was a story of humiliation at the hands of the British.

AFTERWORD

Much has happened in my life since my paternal grandmother told me when I was ten that if I ever shot a policeman, 'Be sure and dig him up and shoot him again, as you can never trust a policeman, alive or dead.' It is only in recent years that I have fully realised why most people reacted with horror whenever I told this story. Back then it was no big deal, it was just something my grandmother said.

Some might say it was a form of child abuse, or is this too strong an accusation? Well, I can still hear my grandmother saying those words, and I did go on to murder a policeman. I am not trying to blame others for what I did – my decisions have always been my own – but my guess is that I was hot-wired for delinquency if the right call came at the right time, as unfortunately it did.

In my experience, those who need a cause find a cause,

and it is this need, coupled with opportunity, that propels these people to act. The more extreme or nihilistic the cause, the fewer the candidates likely to heed the call. But some will, and this is when the true believer comes into his or her own. James Connolly was a true believer of the most extreme kind. Having immersed myself in his life for the last couple of years I can come to no other conclusion.

He was born into a poverty-stricken immigrant community in Little Ireland in Edinburgh that was soaked body and soul in resentment, grievance and victimhood, both real and imagined, and always luxuriated in. There were plenty of old Fenians around to spin tall tales of glorious battles won and lost – and they were tall tales because after 1798 there were no battles worth talking about. Such extreme settings were and always will be a breeding ground for fanaticism, resulting in a desire for revenge and the pursuit of impossible idealistic dreams. Connolly was a very intelligent young man who dreamed of better things, and he followed a well-travelled road when he joined the British Army aged fourteen.

What happened to him in the army is largely unknown, but that he came to hate everything about it is clear from his later writings. It was during this period that he began to read Land League and other Nationalist and radical publications. By the time he deserted and arrived in Dundee he was ready to throw himself into socialist and trade union activity, almost immediately becoming a full-time activist.

For sure he was an extraordinary man, but he was also selfish, arrogant and entirely wilful in the pursuit of his cause. And his cause had to be absolute, one that would create the world anew, one that could convince him that he was sacrificing everything in the selfless pursuit of the betterment of man. He started his adult working life as a dung collector in Edinburgh, but he was also an idealist who was afire with a vision, which was Marxism.

By taking part in the Easter Rising Connolly created a puzzle of contradictions around the future of socialism in Ireland that could never fully be solved. He convinced himself that his participation in the Rising was the right thing to do, perhaps because he just wanted to *do* something. His failure to persuade the working class, his 'revolutionary vanguard', to rally to the cause of socialism rather than die in vast numbers on the Western Front was an ideological and personal affront. He also convinced himself that he could use the much more powerful force of Irish Nationalism to create a road to power for Marxism in Ireland. In this he was proved utterly wrong and it was Irish Catholic Nationalism that emerged triumphant from the Rising and provided the moral framework for the new state that emerged after the Treaty.

In my view, James Connolly's legacy is one of ruined lives and unrealised dreams. For all his abilities as a writer and thinker, it is for his participation in the Rising, and particularly the manner of his execution, that he is honoured and glorified and why he continues to inspire young people today. When John Leslie described the

Rising as 'sad, mad and bad', he could as easily have been looking into the future and describing Connolly's legacy.

For a period in the 1960s, Connolly and his belief system came to represent a bridge between 1916 and a new, forward-looking, pluralist Ireland. You could accommodate 1916, or at least not disown it, by championing the other Connolly – the socialist, the internationalist, the feminist. Then the problems in the North exploded, and all the tensions and contradictions that Connolly represented came home to roost, ultimately resulting in the terrifying factions that became the Provisional IRA, the INLA, the so-called dissident Republicans of our present day, and Connolly House, Sinn Fein's headquarters in Belfast, where people were summoned to account for 'anti-social activities'. This is the harsh reality of his inheritance to us, and nothing that the Irish Labour Party or socialists in Ireland or Britain, as well as some intellectuals and writers, say or do can alter it.

I believe Connolly has nothing to offer the Ireland of today. He was wrong about the nature of Irish society, wrong about the relationship between Ireland and Britain, and he never understood, or made any serious attempt to understand, the true situation in Ulster.

I have thought about Connolly long and hard over the years, debated and argued about him with people from all walks of life while planning and writing this book. I do not hate that child from an Edinburgh slum, yet I deplore his legacy. It is simply not good enough to seek refuge in the facile notion (as some writers continue to do) that he died for Ireland or that he wrote or said some interesting things. There was nothing to stop him living for Ireland and going on to champion the cause of socialism. Too many innocent men and women died for Ireland, without any choice, and I believe that his words and actions contributed to their deaths.

Just as some young Muslims are drawn to a purist and reactionary interpretation of Islam, there are still young men and women today who are being duped by a purist and reactionary narrative of Ireland's humiliation at the hands of its ancient enemy. These are powerful forces for fanaticism, kept alive by songs and poems, stories and myths, nourished by some who should know better, and peddled by others who are true believers with hate-filled hearts.

As Eric Hoffer pointed out, there are many differences between fanatics, but they also have much in common. No one will ever tackle the problem successfully until they confront these common points and recognise them for what they are. When people say that Islamist jihadists are not Muslims they are talking nonsense. They may not be their kind of Muslim, but they are Muslims nonetheless. The day that a young Muslim joins a murderous jihadi group while professing not to believe in the teachings of Mohammed or the Koran will be the day that a young Irish Nationalist joins the Real IRA while saying James Connolly was wrong and the 1916 Rising was an act of gross delinquency. It is irresponsible to pretend otherwise.

The young men and women who join extremist groups, violent or not, are motivated for a variety of reasons. When I joined the Provisional IRA at fifteen I spent several years entirely convinced that my role in life was to fight and die for my cause. It is a sad fact that there are many young people today prepared to do the same, all of them inspired by a learned history of humiliation and oppression and a rigorous belief system.

There will always be battles to fight and debates to engage in. There will always be people who will rage against intolerance or bigotry and we need all of this as we confront and struggle with the problems we face. Yet there are others who want to destroy everything we believe in, including our existence as individual human beings with consciences and the ability to choose right from wrong. And in my view it is always the true believer who leads this charge.

It is the job of police and security services to deal with the threat of violence. It is our job to create a civic society that will isolate and make ineffective those who want to destroy our way of life.

This is one big ask, and looking back on where I have come from, and with my experiences of good and evil, I can see it requires above all else a firm and unflinching determination to promote the hard-won centuries-old values of liberal democracy. Some value systems are worthier than others and, as we face a complex and uncertain future, it is now more important than ever that we make the right choice.

ACKNOWLEDGEMENTS

This book could not have been written without the active support and many kindnesses shown to me by numerous people over many years. The existence of active terrorist groups who pose an ongoing threat to my life means that it would be unfair and unwise to provide a map of friends, colleagues and associates.

I will therefore confine myself to mentioning those publicly associated with the book or those whose friendship with me is in the public domain.

At the outset I must thank Selina Walker and Century for commissioning the book. Selina was unwavering in her support and it is a testament to her enthusiasm and editorial expertise that the book has finally been completed. I am also very grateful to Kate and Cassandra, in particular, for their enthusiasm, diligence and kindness.

Acknowledgements

Thanks are also due to my agent Peter Robinson for his always helpful advice and support.

A special word of thanks goes to Ruth Dudley Edwards for her friendship, courage, support and advice over many years. This book simply would not have been possible without it.

Henry Robinson has been an incredible friend and comrade for more than twenty years.

Martyn Frampton, as always, was extremely supportive and his advice and contribution were invaluable.

Professor Liam Kennedy has been both a friend and a wonderful ally in tough times.

I would like to thank Professor (Lord) Paul Bew for his friendship, wisdom and brilliant insights.

A big thank you goes to Dean Godson for his friendship and constant support over many years.

I would also like to say thanks to John Bew, Professor Charles Townshend, Douglas Murray, Professor Richard English, John Morrison and Professor John Horgan for their help and encouragement. Thank you also Jason McCue and Bob Geldof.

There are hundreds of others I should say thank you to here but my reason for not doing so will, I hope, be understood. I have not forgotten a single one of you.

SOURCE NOTES

Introduction

1. *Mayo News*, 1 June 1939.
2. Charles Townshend, *Easter 1916: The Irish Rebellion*, Penguin, 2006, p. 98.

Chapter 1

1. Niccolo Machiavelli, *The Prince*, Oxford University Press, second edition, 2005, pp. 6-8
2. Ibid. pp. 6–8.
3. John Hewitt, 'The Glittering Sod', *Freehold and Other Poems*, Blackstaff Press, 1986.
4. A.T.Q. Stewart, *The Narrow Ground: The Roots of Conflict in Ulster*, Faber, 1977, p. 5.
5. Conor Cruise O'Brien, *States of Ireland*, Hutchinson, third edition, 1973, p. 40.

6. Ibid. p. 35.
7. Sean O'Callaghan, *The Informer*, Corgi, 1998, p. 81.

Chapter 2

1. John Symington, *The Working Man's Home*, Edinburgh, 1866, pp. 158–9.
2. Donal Nevin, *James Connolly: A Full Life*, Gill and Macmillan, 2005, p. 30.
3. Ibid. p. 6.
4. Ibid. p. 12.
5. Ibid. p. 12.
6. Ibid. p. 719.

Chapter 3

1. Donal Nevin, *James Connolly: A Full Life*, Gill and Macmillan, 2005, p. 725.
2. Ibid. p. 33.
3. Darrell Figgis, *Recollections of the Irish War*, Garden City, New York, Doubleday, 1927, pp. 86–7.
4. Donal Nevin, *James Connolly: A Full Life*, Gill and Macmillan, 2005, p. 724.
5. Ibid. p. 34.
6. Ibid. p. 44.
7. Ibid. p. 44.
8. John Leslie, *Justice*, 14 December 1895.
9. *The Harp*, March 1908.
10. Fearghal McGarry, *The Rising: Ireland: Easter 1916*, Oxford University Press, 2011, pp. 20–1.

11. By kind permission of the Estate of Sean O'Casey, Sean O'Casey, *Pictures in the Hallway*, Pan Macmillan, 1971.

12. Donal Nevin, *James Connolly: A Full Life*, Gill and Macmillan, 2005, pp. 76–7.

13. Samuel Levenson, *James Connolly: A Biography*, Martin Brian and O'Keeffe, 1973, p. 103.

14. Donal Nevin, *James Connolly: A Full Life*, Gill and Macmillan, 2005, pp. 217–18.

15. James Stevenson, *Clashing Personalities: James Connolly and Daniel De Leon, 1896-1909*, Eire-Ireland, 1990.

16. Elizabeth Gurley Flynn, *I Speak My Own Piece*, Masses and Mainstream, 1955, p. 86.

17. *New York Post*, 27 May 1916.

18. Donal Nevin, *James Connolly: A Full Life*, Gill and Macmillan, 2005, p. 313.

19. Ibid. p. 218.

Chapter 4

1. *Liberty Magazine*, Dublin, April 1966.

2. Emmet Larkin, *James Larkin: Irish Labour Leader 1876–1947*, Routledge Kegan Paul, 1965, p. 138.

3. Donal Nevin, *James Connolly: A Full Life*, Gill and Macmillan, 2005, p. 484.

4. Samuel Levenson, *James Connolly: A Biography*, Martin Brian and O'Keeffe, 1973, p. 240.

5. Conor Cruise O'Brien, *States of Ireland*, Hutchinson, 1973, p. 47.

6. Fearghal McGarry, *The Rising: Ireland: Easter 1916*, Oxford University Press, 2011, p. 92.

Chapter 5

1. Desmond Ryan, *The Rising: The Complete Story of Easter Week*, Golden Eagle Books, 1949, p. 49.
2. Donal Nevin, *James Connolly: A Full Life*, Gill and Macmillan, 2005, p. 631.
3. Darrell Figgis, *Recollections of the Irish War*, Doubleday, 1927, pp. 86–7.
4. John Francis Byrne, *Silent Years*, Octagon Books, 1975.
5. Fearghal McGarry, *The Rising: Ireland: Easter 1916*, Oxford University Press, 2011, p. 177.
6. James Stephens, *The Insurrection in Dublin*, Maunsel and Co., 1916, p. 74.
7. Samuel Levenson, *James Connolly: A Biography*, Martin Brian and O'Keeffe, 1973, p. 308.
8. Max Caulfield, *The Easter Rebellion*, Frederick Muller Ltd, 1964, p. 349.
9. Donal Nevin, *James Connolly: A Full Life*, Gill and Macmillan, 2005, p. 679.
10. Ibid. p. 667.

Chapter 6

1. *The Voice of Labour*, 10 May 1919.
2. Donal Nevin, *James Connolly: A Full Life*, Gill and Macmillan, 2005, p. 707.
3. Michael T. Foy and Brian Barton, *The Easter Rising*, History Press, 2011, p. 224.

4. James Stephens, *The Insurrection in Dublin*, Maunsel and Co., 1916, p. 47.
5. Michael T. Foy and Brian Barton, *The Easter Rising*, History Press, 2011, p. 227.
6. Charles Townshend, *Easter 1916: The Irish Rebellion*, Penguin, 2006, p. 180.
7. Ibid. p. 281.
8. Ibid. pp. 281–2.
9. W. K. Anderson, *James Connolly and the Irish Left*, Irish Academic Press, 1994, p. 96.
10. Richard English, *Armed Struggle: A History of the IRA*, Pan Macmillan, 2004, p. 17.
11. Richard English, *Irish Freedom: The History of Nationalism in Ireland*, Pan Macmillan, 2007, p. 308.
12. Michael Laffan, *Judging W.T. Cosgrave*, Royal Irish Academy, 2014, p. 124.

Chapter 7

1. Brian Hughes, *16 Lives: Michael Mallin*, O'Brien Press, 2012, pp. 178–9.
2. William Patrick Ryan, *The Irish Labour Movement*, BW Huebsch Incorporated, 1920, p. 286.
3. Conor Cruise O'Brien, *States of Ireland*, Hutchinson, 1973, p. 111.
4. Michael Laffan, *Judging W.T. Cosgrave*, Royal Irish Academy, 2014, p. 128.
5. Ibid. p. 209.
6. W.K. Anderson, *James Connolly and the Irish Left*, Irish Academic Press, 1994, p. 93.

7. Richard English, *Irish Freedom: The History of Nationalism in Ireland*, Pan Macmillan, 2007, p. 339.
8. The IRA's *War News*, 16 November 1940.

Chapter 8

1. Tim Pat Coogan, *The IRA*, HarperCollins, 1987, pp. 164–5.
2. George Orwell, 'Notes on Nationalism', *Polemic*, extract from the *Observer*, May 1945.
3. Matt Treacy, *The Communist Party of Ireland 1921–2011*, Brocaire Books, 2013, p. 149.

Chapter 9

1. Dermot Keogh, *Twentieth-Century Ireland: Nation and State*, Gill and Macmillian, 1994, p. 253.
2. Brian Hanley and Scott Millar, *The Lost Revolution: The Story of the Official IRA and the Workers' Party*, Penguin, 2010, p. 28.
3. Ibid. p. 29.
4. Richard English, *Armed Struggle: A History of the IRA*, Pan Macmillan, 2004, p. 84.
5. Dermot Keogh, *Twentieth-Century Ireland: Nation and State*, Gill and Macmillan, 1994, p. 259.
6. Michael O'Sullivan, *Sean Lemass: A Biography*, Blackwater Press, 1994, p. 185.
7. *The Collected Poems of John Hewitt*, Frank Ormsby Black staff Press, Belfast 1991.

Chapter 10

1. Clair Wills, *Dublin 1916: The Siege of the GPO*, Profile Books, 2009, p. 191.
2. Roisin Higgins, *Transforming 1916: Meaning, Memory and the Fiftieth Anniversary of the Easter Rising*, Cork University Press, 2012, p. 22.
3. Ibid. pp. 27–8.
4. Ibid. pp. 1–2.
5. Ibid. p. 71.
6. Bob Purdie, *Politics in the Streets: The Origins of the Civil Rights Movement in Northern Ireland*, Blackstaff Press, 1990, p. 31.

Chapter 11

1. Conor Cruise O'Brien, *States of Ireland*, Hutchinson, 1973, p. 191.

Chapter 13

1. Jack Holland and Henry McDonald, *INLA: Deadly Divisions*, Torc, 1994, p. 32.
2. *The Irish Times*, 14th December 1974.

Chapter 14

1. Fearghal McGarry (ed.), *Republicanism in Modern Ireland*, University College Dublin Press, 2003, p. 3.
2. Sean O'Casey, *The Shadow of a Gunman*, first performed in the Abbey Theatre, Dublin, 1923.

3. Nora Connolly O'Brien, *We Shall Rise Again*, Mosquito Press, 1981, p. 40.
4. Ibid. p. 117.
5. 'They Shoot Children, Don't They?', a report by Professor Liam Kennedy, Queen's University Belfast.
6. Richard English, *Armed Struggle: A History of the IRA*, Macmillan, 2004, p. 236.

Chapter 15

1. Eric Hoffer, *The True Believer*, Harper Perennial Modern Classics, 2009 (first published in 1951), preface.
2. Ibid.
3. Vaclav Havel, *Disturbing the Peace: A Conversation with Karel Hvizdala*, Faber, 1990, pp. 178–80.

BIBLIOGRAPHY

The following sources have been used in the making of this book. Some I have quoted from, others have provided guidance and context, all have proved invaluable.

Adams, Gerry, *The Politics of Irish Freedom*, Bron Books, 1986

Anderson, W.K., *James Connolly and the Irish Left*, Irish Academic Press, 1994

Bardon, Jonathan, *A History of Ulster*, Blackstaff Press, 1992

Barton, Brian, *From Behind a Closed Door: Secret Court Martial Records of the 1916 Rising*, Blackstaff Press, 2002

Bew, Paul, *Conflict and Conciliation in Ireland 1890–1910*, Clarendon Press, 1987

Bew, Paul, *Ireland and the Politics of Enmity 1789–2006*, Oxford University Press, 2006

Bew, Paul, Peter Gibbon and Henry Patterson, *The State in Northern Ireland 1921–72*, St Martin's Press, 1979

Byrne, John Francis, *Silent Years*, Octagon Books, 1975

Caulfield, Max, *The Easter Rebellion*, Frederick Muller Ltd, 1964

Collins, Lorcan, *James Connolly*, The O'Brien Press, 2013

Connolly, James, *Collected Works* (two volumes), New Books, 1987

Connolly O'Brien, Nora, *James Connolly: Portrait of a Rebel Father*, Dublin, Four Masters, 1975

Connolly O'Brien, Nora, *We Shall Rise Again*, Mosquito Press, 1981

Coogan, Tim Pat, *The IRA*, HarperCollins, 1987

Edwards, Owen Dudley, *The Mind of an Activist: James Connolly*, Gill and Macmillan, 1971

Edwards, Owen Dudley and Bernard Ransom (eds), *James Connolly: Selected Political Writings*, Jonathan Cape, 1973

Edwards, Ruth Dudley, *James Connolly*, Gill and Macmillan, 1980

Edwards, Ruth Dudley, *Patrick Pearse: The Triumph of Failure*, Poolbeg, 1990

Edwards, Ruth Dudley and Bridget, Hourican, *An Atlas of Irish History*, Routledge, 2005

English, Richard, *Armed Struggle: A History of the IRA*, Pan Macmillan, 2004

English, Richard, *Irish Freedom*: *The History of Nationalism in Ireland*, Pan Macmillan, 2007

Enright, Sean, *Easter Rising 1916: The Trial*, Merrion Press, 2014

Fanning, Ronan, *Fatal Path: British Government and Irish Revolution, 1910–1922*, Faber & Faber, 2013

Figgis, Darrell, *Recollections of the Irish War*, Doubleday, 1927

FitzGerald, Desmond, *Memoirs of Desmond FitzGerald 1913–1916*, Routledge & Kegan Paul, 1968

Fitzpatrick, David, *Politics and Irish Life, 1913–1921: Provincial Experience of War and Revolution*, Gill and Macmillan, 1977

Foster, R.F., *Vivid Faces: The Revolutionary Generation in Ireland, 1890–1923*, Allen Lane, 2014

Foy, Michael T. and Brian Barton, *The Easter Rising*, History Press, 2011

Frampton, Martyn, *Legion of the Rearguard: Dissident Irish Republicanism*, Irish Academic Press, 2011

Frampton, Martyn, *The Long March: The Political Strategy of Sinn Fein, 1981–2007*, Palgrave Macmillan, 2009

Greaves, C. Desmond, *The Life and Times of James Connolly*, Lawrence & Wishart, 1961

Gurley Flynn, Elizabeth, *I Speak My Own Piece*, Masses and Mainstream, 1955

Hanley, Brian and Scott Millar, *The Lost Revolution: The Story of the Official IRA and the Workers' Party*, Penguin, 2010

Havel, Vaclav, *Disturbing the Peace: A Conversation with Karel Hvizdala*, Faber & Faber, 1990

Hewitt, John, *Freehold and Other Poems*, Blackstaff Press, 1986

Higgins, Roisin, *Transforming 1916: Meaning, Memory and the Fiftieth Anniversary of the Easter Rising*, Cork University Press, 2012

Hoffer, Eric, *The True Believer*, HarperCollins (Perennial Modern Classics), 2009

Holland, Jack and Henry McDonald, *INLA: Deadly Divisions*, Torc, 1994

Horgan, John, *Divided We Stand: The Strategy and Psychology of Ireland's Dissident Terrorists*, Oxford University Press, 2013

Hughes, Brian, *16 Lives: Michael Mallin*, O'Brien Press, 2012

Inglis, Brian, *Roger Casement*, Purnell Book Services, 1973

Justice, 14 December 1898

Kennedy, Liam, *A Most Oppressed People: Essays in Modern Irish History*, Irish Academic Press, 2012

Kennedy, Liam, 'They Shoot Children, Don't They?', Queen's University Belfast, 2001

Keogh, Dermot, *Twentieth-Century Ireland; Nation and State*, Gill and Macmillan, 1994

Laffan, Michael, *Judging W.T. Cosgrave*, Royal Irish Academy, 2014

Larkin, Emmet, *James Larkin: Irish Labour Leader 1876–1947*, Routledge & Kegan Paul, 1965

Lawlor, Sheila, *Britain and Ireland: 1914–1923*, Gill and Macmillan, 1983

Levenson, Samuel, *James Connolly: A Biography*, Martin Brian and O'Keeffe, 1973

Liberty Magazine, Dublin, April 1966

Lyons, F.S.L., *Culture and Anarchy in Ireland, 1890–1939*, Oxford University Press, 1979

Machiavelli, Niccolo, *The Prince*, Oxford University Press, second edition, 2005

Martin, F.X. (ed.), *Leaders and Men of the Easter Rising: Dublin 1916*, Methuen & Co., 1967

McCoole, Sinéad, *Easter Widows: Seven Irish Women Who Lived in the Shadow of the 1916 Rising*, Doubleday Ireland, 2014

McCormack, W.J., *Dublin 1916: The French Connection*, Gill and Macmillan, 2012

McGarry, Fearghal, *Rebels: Voices from the Easter Rising*, Penguin, 2012

McGarry, Fearghal (ed.), *Republicanism in Modern Ireland*, University College Dublin Press, 2003

McGarry, Fearghal, *The Rising: Easter 1916*, Oxford University Press, 2011

McGladdery, Gary, *The Provisional IRA in England: The Bombing Campaign, 1973–1997*, Irish Academic Press, 2006

McHugh, Roger (ed.), *Dublin 1916*, Arlington Books, 1966

McIntyre, Anthony, *Good Friday: The Death of Irish Republicanism*, Ausubo Press, 2008

McKearney, Tommy, *The Provisional IRA – From Insurrection to Parliament*, Pluto Press, 2011

Morgan, Austen, *James Connolly: A Political Biography*, Manchester University Press, 1988

Morrison, John F., *The Origins and Rise of Dissident Republicanism: The Role and Impact of Organisational Splits*, Bloomsbury, 2013

Nevin, Donal, *James Connolly: A Full Life*, Gill and Macmillan, 2005

New York Post, 27 May 1916

O'Brien, Conor Cruise (ed.), *The Shaping of Modern Ireland*, Routledge & Kegan Paul, 1960

O'Brien, Conor Cruise, *States of Ireland*, Hutchinson, third edition, 1973

O'Brien, William and Desmond Ryan (eds), *Devoy's Post Bag*, Vol. II, 1871–1928, C.J. Fallon, 1953

O' Callaghan, Sean, *The Informer*, Corgi, 1998

O'Casey, Sean, *Autobiographies I*, Pan Macmillan, 1972

O'Casey, Sean, *Pictures in the Hallway*, Pan Macmillan, 1971

O'Casey, Sean, *The Story of the Irish Citizen Army*, The Journeyman Press, 1919

O'Doherty, Malachi, *The Trouble With Guns: Republican Strategy and the Provisional IRA*, Blackstaff Press, 1999

O'Faolain, Sean, *Constance Markievicz*, Jonathan Cape, 1934

O'Malley, Ernie (edited by Cormac K.H.O'Malley and Tim Horgan), *The Men Will Talk to Me: Kerry Interviews:* Mercier Press, 2012

O'Malley, Ernie, *The Singing Flame*, Anvil Books, 1978

O'Rawe, Richard, *Blanketmen*, 2005

Orwell, George, 'Notes on Nationalism', *Polemic*, May 1945

O'Sullivan, Michael, *Sean Lemass: A Biography*, Blackwater Press, 1994

Pantucci, Raffaello, 'We love death as you love life', *Britain's Suburban Terrorists*, Hurst and Company, 2015

Patterson, Henry, *The Politics of Illusion: A Political History of the IRA*, Serif, 1997

Prince, Simon, *Northern Ireland's '68, Civil Rights, Global, Revolt and the Origins of the Troubles*, Irish Academic Press, 2007

Prince, Simon and Warner, Geoffrey, *Belfast and Derry in Revolt: A New History of the Start of the Troubles*, Irish Academic Press, 2012

Purdie, Bob, *Politics in the Streets: The Origins of the Civil Rights Movement in Northern Ireland*, Blackstaff Press, 1990

Rafter, Kevin, *Sinn Fein, 1905–2005*, Gill and Macmillan, 2005

Regan, John M., *Myth and the Irish State*, Irish Academic Press, 2013

Ryan, Desmond, *The Rising: The Complete Story of Easter Week*, Golden Eagle Books, 1949

Ryan, William Patrick, *The Irish Labour Movement*, BW Huebsch Incorporated, 1920

Sorohan, Sean, *Irish London During the Troubles*, Irish Academic Press, 2012

Stephens, James, *The Insurrection in Dublin*, Maunsel and Co., 1916

Stern, Jessica, *Terror in the Name of God*, HarperCollins, 2003

Stevenson, James, *Clashing Personalities: James Connolly and Daniel De Leon, 1896–1909*, Eire-Ireland, 1990

Stewart, A.T.Q., *The Narrow Ground: The Roots of Conflict in Ulster*, Faber & Faber, 1977

Symington, John, *The Working Man's Home*, Edinburgh, 1866

The Voice of Labour, 10 May 1919

Thompson, William Irwin, *The Imagination of an Insurrection: Dublin, Easter 1916; A Study of an Ideological Movement*, Harper Colophon Books, 1972

Tierney, Michael (edited by F. X. Martin), *Eoin MacNeill: Scholar and Man of Action, 1867–1945*, Clarendon Press, 1980

Toolis, Kevin, *Rebel Hearts, Journeys Within the IRA's Soul*, Picador, 1995

Townshend, Charles, *Easter 1916: The Irish Rebellion*, Penguin, 2006

Treacy, Matt, *The Communist Party of Ireland, 1921–2011*, Brocaire Books, 2013

The Harp, March 1908

War News, 16 November 1940

Wills, Clair, *Dublin 1916: The Siege of the GPO*, Profile Books, 2009

Yeats, Padraig, *A City in Wartime, Dublin, 1914–1918*, Gill and Macmillan, 2011

Yeats, Padraig, *Lockout Dublin 1913: The Most Famous Labour Dispute in Irish History*, St Martin's Press, 2001

INDEX